First World War
and Army of Occupation
War Diary
France, Belgium and Germany

38 DIVISION
Divisional Troops
123 Field Company Royal Engineers
1 December 1915 - 7 June 1919

WO95/2547/1

The Naval & Military Press Ltd
www.nmarchive.com
Published in association with The National Archives

Published by

The Naval & Military Press Ltd

Unit 10 Ridgewood Industrial Park,

Uckfield, East Sussex,

TN22 5QE England

Tel: +44 (0) 1825 749494

www.naval-military-press.com

www.nmarchive.com

This diary has been reprinted in facsimile from the original. Any imperfections are inevitably reproduced and the quality may fall short of modern type and cartographic standards.

© Crown Copyright
Images reproduced by permission of The National Archives, London, England, 2015.

Contents

Document type	Place/Title	Date From	Date To
Miscellaneous	WO95/2547/1 123 Field Company Royal Engineers		
Heading	123rd Field Coy R.E. Dec 1915-Jun 1919		
Heading	War Diary Of 123rd Field Co. Royal Engineers. From 1st Dec.1915 To 31st Dec 1915. Volume One.		
Heading	38th Div 123rd F.C.R.E. Dec 15 June 19		
War Diary	Winchester	01/12/1915	01/12/1915
War Diary	Southampton	01/12/1915	01/12/1915
War Diary	Havre	02/12/1915	03/12/1915
War Diary	St Omer	04/12/1915	04/12/1915
War Diary	Mametz	05/12/1915	10/12/1915
War Diary	Lavantie	11/12/1915	11/12/1915
War Diary	Le Sart	20/12/1915	31/12/1915
Heading	123rd F.C.R.E. Vol. 2		
War Diary	Le Sart	01/01/1916	11/01/1916
War Diary	La Couture	12/01/1916	31/01/1916
Miscellaneous	A.G's. Office. Base.	01/03/1916	01/03/1916
War Diary	La Couture	01/02/1916	17/02/1916
War Diary	Le Touret	18/02/1916	29/02/1916
Miscellaneous	O.C. 123rd Field Co. R.E.		
War Diary	Le Touret X15.d.8.2	01/03/1916	31/03/1916
Miscellaneous	123rd Field Company Royal Engineers.	03/05/1916	03/05/1916
War Diary	Le Touret X.15.d.8.2	01/04/1916	15/04/1916
War Diary	Estaires	16/04/1916	16/04/1916
War Diary	R12.C.6.5	17/04/1916	17/04/1916
War Diary	Levantie M9.b.6.9	18/04/1916	30/04/1916
War Diary	Laventie	01/05/1916	15/06/1916
War Diary	Abbeye Neuvelle Ferme	16/06/1916	26/06/1916
War Diary	Monchel	27/06/1916	27/06/1916
War Diary	Ribeaucourt	28/06/1916	30/06/1916
Heading	War Diary of 123rd Field Coy R.E. 38th Welsh Div July 1916 Vol 8		
War Diary	Puchevillers	01/07/1916	01/07/1916
War Diary	Toutencourt	02/07/1916	03/07/1916
War Diary	Mericourt L'Abbe	04/07/1916	05/07/1916
War Diary	F.28.b.17	06/07/1916	20/07/1916
War Diary	Rossignal Farm	21/07/1916	22/07/1916
War Diary	Colincamps	23/07/1916	31/07/1916
War Diary	Ledringhem	31/07/1916	31/07/1916
Heading	War Diary August 1916. 123rd Field Company Royal Engineers. Vol 9		
War Diary	Ledringhem	01/08/1916	03/08/1916
War Diary	Bavinchove	03/08/1916	03/08/1916
War Diary	Caestre	04/08/1916	22/08/1916
War Diary	C.25.d.0.7. near Ypres	23/08/1916	31/08/1916
Heading	War Diary 123rd Field Coy RE September 1916 Vol 10		
War Diary	C25 d07 near Ypres	01/09/1916	30/09/1916
Heading	Original War Diary-October-1916. 123 Field Coy. R.E. 38th (Welsh) Dvn. 31-10-1916 Vol II		
War Diary	C25d07 Ypres	01/10/1916	31/10/1916

Heading	War Diary-November 1916. 123rd Field Coy, Royal Engineers 38th (Welsh) Division 1.12.16 Vol 12		
War Diary	C25 d.0.7. Ypres	01/11/1916	30/11/1916
Miscellaneous	H.Q. 114th Brigade	18/11/1916	18/11/1916
Diagram etc	Reinforced Concrete Machine Gun Emplacement.		
Diagram etc	Reinforced Concrete Dugout & O.P. Height Inside 5'-0" Roof total thickness 4'-0" Position of charges shown thus		
Diagram etc	Section of German Parapet.		
Diagram etc	Concrete O.P.		
Heading	War Diary-December 1916 123rd Field Co. Royal Engineers 38th (Welsh) Division Vol 13 31.12.1916		
War Diary	Ypres C25d07	01/12/1916	11/12/1916
War Diary	A.18.b.2.8	12/12/1916	31/12/1916
Heading	War Diary-January 1917. 123rd Field Co, Royal Engrs. 38th (Welsh) Division Vol 14		
War Diary	Watten France	01/01/1917	11/01/1917
War Diary	C.25.d.0.7. Ypres	12/01/1917	31/01/1917
Heading	War Diary-February 1917. 123rd Field Co. Royal Engineers 38th (Welsh) Division Vol 15		
War Diary	C.25.d.07. Ypres	01/02/1917	22/02/1917
War Diary	Hill Top Sector	23/02/1917	28/02/1917
Heading	War Diary-March 1917. 123rd Field Co. Royal Engineers 38th (Welsh) Division Vol 16		
War Diary	C25 d 0.7. Canal Bank N. of Ypres	01/03/1917	06/03/1917
War Diary	C 25d0 7 Ypres	07/03/1917	31/03/1917
Heading	War Diary-April 1917 123 Field Co. Royal Engrs. 38 (Welsh) Division. Vol 17		
War Diary	Ypres Hilltop Sector	01/04/1917	17/04/1917
War Diary	Ypres Canal Bank E Side near Bridge 3.b	18/04/1917	30/04/1917
Heading	Original War Diary May-1917 123rd Field Company R.E. Vol 18		
War Diary	Ypres. Canal Bank. E. Side near Bridge 3.b.	01/05/1917	29/05/1917
War Diary	Billets in Watten	30/05/1917	31/05/1917
Heading	War Diary-June 1917 123rd-Field Coy, Royal Engineers 38th (Welsh) Division. Vol 19		
War Diary	Watten	01/06/1917	12/06/1917
War Diary	Watten To Canal Bank N of B14 N of Ypres	13/06/1917	13/06/1917
War Diary	N. of Ypres N of Br 4 Over Yser Canal	14/06/1917	17/06/1917
War Diary	Yser Canal W Bank N of Ypres	18/06/1917	30/06/1917
Heading	War Diary-July 1917. 123 Field Co Royal Engineers 38 (Welsh) Division Vol 20		
War Diary	Yser Canal W Bank N of Ypres between Bridge 4 & Bridge 5	01/07/1917	02/07/1917
War Diary	Yser Canal W. Bank	03/07/1917	21/07/1917
War Diary	G. Camp	22/07/1917	24/07/1917
War Diary	Dragon Camp Wood	25/07/1917	31/07/1917
Heading	War Diary 123rd Field Company, Royal Engineers-38th (Welsh) Division August 1917 Vol 21		
War Diary	Canal Bank N of Ypres	01/08/1917	05/08/1917
War Diary	Cardoen Farm	06/08/1917	19/08/1917
War Diary	HQ & Nos 2&3 Section B 23 Central	20/08/1917	21/08/1917
War Diary	Bivouacs B 23 Central near L 2	22/08/1917	22/08/1917
War Diary	N of Ypres With Two Sections at	23/08/1917	23/08/1917
War Diary	Cardoen Farm Working at	24/08/1917	24/08/1917
War Diary	Re Dump On Dank	25/08/1917	25/08/1917

War Diary	Horselines W of Dawsons Corner	26/08/1917	28/08/1917
War Diary	HQ & 3 Sections B 23 Central	29/08/1917	31/08/1917
Heading	War Diary September 1917. 123rd Field Co. Royal Engineers. 38th (Welsh) Division. Vol 22		
War Diary	H.Q. & 3 Sections at B. 23 Central	01/09/1917	07/09/1917
War Diary	Cardoen Farm.	08/09/1917	10/09/1917
War Diary	Salem Camp. near Crombeck	11/09/1917	12/09/1917
War Diary	Erquingham	18/09/1917	22/09/1917
War Diary	Salem Camp near Crombeck	13/09/1917	13/09/1917
War Diary	Crombeck to Eeke	14/09/1917	14/09/1917
War Diary	Eeke to Morbeke	15/09/1917	15/09/1917
War Diary	Morbeke to Estaires	16/09/1917	16/09/1917
War Diary	Estaires to Erquingham	17/09/1917	30/09/1917
War Diary	Erquinghem Laundry	01/10/1917	31/10/1917
Heading	War Diary Novr 1917 123 Field Coy. R.E. 38 (Welsh) Division Vol 24		
War Diary	Erquinghem Laundry	01/11/1917	25/11/1917
War Diary	Jute Factory Armentieres	26/11/1917	30/11/1917
Heading	War Diary-January 1918 123 Field Comp. Royal Engineers 38th (Welsh) Division		
Heading	War Diary-December 1917.123rd Field Co. Royal Engineers Vol 25		
War Diary	Jute Factory Armentieres	01/12/1917	19/12/1917
War Diary	G.17.a.9.2. Sheet 36	20/12/1917	29/12/1917
War Diary	Fort Rompu.	30/12/1917	12/01/1918
War Diary	Rue Dormoire	13/01/1918	14/01/1918
War Diary	Rue Dormoire Move To Old House Lines near Fort Rompu	15/01/1918	15/01/1918
War Diary	Move To La. Have Fam.	16/01/1918	16/01/1918
War Diary	La Haye Farm Near Pont De Nieppe	17/01/1918	24/01/1918
War Diary	La Haye Farm	25/01/1918	31/01/1918
War Diary	La Haye Farm Near Pont De Nieppe	01/02/1918	12/02/1918
War Diary	Pont De Nieppe	15/02/1918	28/02/1918
Heading	War Diary-March 1918 123 Field Company. Royal Engineers 38 (Welsh) Division		
War Diary	Pont De Nieppe	01/03/1918	30/03/1918
War Diary	Le Trou Bayard	31/03/1918	31/03/1918
Heading	38th Div. V. Corps. 123rd Field Company, R.E. April 1918		
War Diary	Trou Bayard	01/04/1918	01/04/1918
War Diary	Merville in Train & Mondicourt March To	02/04/1918	02/04/1918
War Diary	Toutencourt	03/04/1918	04/04/1918
War Diary	Toutencourt To Warloy	05/04/1918	10/04/1918
War Diary	Warloy-Baillon	10/04/1918	11/04/1918
War Diary	Senlis	12/04/1918	16/04/1918
War Diary	Senlis V.15.6.2.8 Sheet 57D S.E.	17/04/1918	18/04/1918
War Diary	Contay	19/04/1918	19/04/1918
War Diary	Senlis	20/04/1918	24/04/1918
War Diary	Toutencourt	25/04/1918	25/04/1918
War Diary	Senlis	26/04/1918	26/04/1918
War Diary	Toutencourt	27/04/1918	30/04/1918
Heading	War Diary May 1918 123 Field Coy. Royal Engineers 38th (Welsh) Division.		
War Diary	Toutencourt To V.8.a.7.7	01/05/1918	04/05/1918
War Diary	V 8 a 7 7 near Warloy-Hedauville Road.	05/05/1918	15/05/1918
War Diary	V.8.a.7.7	16/05/1918	17/05/1918

War Diary	To V.5.a. Bluff Near Hedauville Wood	18/05/1918	20/05/1918
War Diary	To Prisoners Of War Cage Toutencourt	20/05/1918	20/05/1918
War Diary	Prisoners Of War Camp Toutencourt	21/05/1918	31/05/1918
Miscellaneous	Programme of Training-123rd Field Co. R.E.		
Heading	War Diary. June. 1918 123 Field Coy. R.E. 38 (Welsh) Divn Vol 31		
War Diary	Toutencourt	01/06/1918	07/06/1918
War Diary	Englebelmer	08/06/1918	11/06/1918
War Diary	Forceville	12/06/1918	30/06/1918
Heading	War Diary. 123 Field Compy Royal Engineers 38 (Welsh) Division		
War Diary	Forceville	01/07/1918	19/07/1918
War Diary	Toutencourt	20/07/1918	31/07/1918
Heading	War Diary August 1918 123 Field Coy R.E. 38th Division Vol 33		
War Diary	Forceville	01/08/1918	02/08/1918
War Diary	Sappers Valley Nr Headauville.	03/08/1918	22/08/1918
War Diary	114 Bn HQ. Engelbelmer	22/08/1918	22/08/1918
War Diary	South Causeway	22/08/1918	23/08/1918
War Diary	Authville Crossing	23/08/1918	23/08/1918
War Diary	Hamel Mill	22/08/1918	23/08/1918
War Diary	North Causeway	23/04/1918	23/04/1918
War Diary	Ancre Valley	24/08/1918	24/08/1918
War Diary	Sapper Valley To "C" Type Shelters East of Engelbelmer	24/08/1918	24/08/1918
War Diary	Authville Crossing	25/08/1918	29/08/1918
War Diary	Pioneer Road	30/08/1918	30/08/1918
War Diary	Pioneer Road	31/08/1918	31/08/1918
Diagram etc	Plan of Autmuille Bridge & Causeway Q 35.d.5.8 to Q 36.c.1.7. Sheet 57D		
Heading	War Diary 123rd Field Co R.E. From 1st September 1918 To 30th September 1918 Vol 34		
War Diary	Longeval	01/09/1918	03/09/1918
War Diary	Sailly-Saillisel	03/09/1918	03/09/1918
War Diary	Sailly	04/09/1918	04/09/1918
War Diary	Etricourt Manancourt	05/09/1918	05/09/1918
War Diary	Etricourt	05/09/1918	05/09/1918
War Diary	Manancourt	05/09/1918	05/09/1918
War Diary	Sailly	05/09/1918	06/09/1918
War Diary	Longueval	07/09/1918	08/09/1918
War Diary	Beaulencourt	09/09/1918	11/09/1918
War Diary	East of Le Chelle	12/09/1918	16/09/1918
War Diary	Lechelle	17/09/1918	27/09/1918
War Diary	Heudicourt	28/09/1918	30/09/1918
Diagram etc	Plan Of Lattice Girder Bridge Over Canal Du Nord At V.8.c.4.0		
Miscellaneous	E Abutment Damaged		
Miscellaneous	To/O.C. 123 Field Cops		
Diagram etc	Canal Du Nord Plan Of Bridge At V 8.b.35.50		
Diagram etc	Rough Sketch of Bridge		
Miscellaneous	To. O.C. 123 Field Coy R.E.		
Heading	War Diary. October 1918. 123rd Field Company R.E. 38th (Welsh) Division		
War Diary	In The Field.	01/10/1918	31/10/1918
Miscellaneous	To Accompany War Diary Of 123 Field Co. RE-October 1918 Appendix "A".		

Diagram etc	To Accompany War Diary 123 Field Co RE-October 1918 Appendix "A"		
War Diary	War Diary November 1st To November 30 1918 123 Field Company RE.		
War Diary	Field	01/11/1918	27/11/1918
War Diary	In The Field	28/11/1918	30/11/1918
Heading	War Diary-December 1918. 123 Field Coy. Royal Engineers 38 (Welsh) Division. Vol 37		
War Diary	Berlaimont	01/12/1918	02/12/1918
War Diary	Salesches	03/12/1918	03/12/1918
War Diary	Villers Bretteneux	04/12/1918	04/12/1918
War Diary	Franvillers	05/12/1918	12/12/1918
War Diary	Warloy	13/12/1918	31/12/1918
Heading	War Diary-Jan. 1919. 123 Field Coy. Royal Engineers 38 (Welsh) Division Vol 38		
War Diary	Warloy	01/01/1918	31/01/1918
Heading	9 Unit 123 Field Coy RE War Diary For Month Of February Vol 39		
War Diary	Warloy	01/02/1919	28/02/1919
Heading	War Diary of 123 Field Coy RE For Month of March 1919 Vol 40		
War Diary	Daours France.	01/03/1919	30/04/1919
War Diary	Daours	01/05/1919	07/06/1919

WO95/2547/1

123 Field Company.
Royal Engineers

38TH DIVISION
DIVL ENGINEERS

123RD FIELD COY R.E.
DEC 1915 - JUN 1919.

Original

CONFIDENTIAL.

WAR DIARY

OF

123RD FIELD CO.

ROYAL ENGINEERS.

FROM 1st DEC. 1915 TO 31st DEC 1915.

VOLUME ONE.

Dec '15
June '19

123rd HCRE
Vol I

131/7936

Army Form C. 2118

WAR DIARY
~~INTELLIGENCE SUMMARY~~
(Erase heading not required.)

Place	Date	Hour	Summary of Events and Information	Remarks and references to Appendices
Winchester	1st Dec 1915.	7.00 am	The company left Avington Park Camp fully mobilized less one sapper under the command of Major S.W. Lamonby R.E. and marched under orders of the G.O.C. 113rd Brigade to Southampton and embarked on board the S.S. City of Chester	
Southampton	"	5 pm.	Sailed from Southampton	
			Weather. Rained practically all day.	
				JWL

Army Form C. 2118

WAR DIARY
or
INTELLIGENCE SUMMARY
(Erase heading not required.)

Instructions regarding War Diaries and Intelligence Summaries are contained in F. S. Regs., Part II. and the Staff Manual respectively. Title Pages will be prepared in manuscript.

Place	Date	Hour	Summary of Events and Information	Remarks and references to Appendices
Havre.	2/12/15	3 a.m.	Arrived outside Havre Harbour.	
		6 a.m.	Docked & started disembarkation.	
		12 noon	Completed disembarkation & marched to No 5 Docks Base Camp.	
			Weather very wet.	

1875 Wt. W593/826 1,000,000 4/15 J.B.C. & A. A.D.S.S./Forms/C. 2118.

Army Form C. 2118

WAR DIARY
or
INTELLIGENCE SUMMARY
(Erase heading not required.)

Instructions regarding War Diaries and Intelligence Summaries are contained in F. S. Regs., Part II. and the Staff Manual respectively. Title Pages will be prepared in manuscript.

Place	Date	Hour	Summary of Events and Information	Remarks and references to Appendices
Havre.	3/12/15	3-30am	Reveille	
		4-30am	Marched to No 3 Point and entrained	
		8-25am	Train left Havre.	
		1-17pm	Train stopped at Bucky for 50 minutes for dinner.	
		6-5pm	Train stopped at Abbeville for 40 minutes for supper.	
			Weather wet.	

Army Form C. 2118

WAR DIARY
or
INTELLIGENCE SUMMARY

(Erase heading not required.)

Instructions regarding War Diaries and Intelligence Summaries are contained in F.S. Regs., Part II. and the Staff Manual respectively. Title Pages will be prepared in manuscript.

Place	Date	Hour	Summary of Events and Information	Remarks and references to Appendices
St Omer	4/12/15	4.00am	Arrived St Omer and detrained	
		7.30am	Marched to Mametz 11 miles south of St Omer and billeted in the village. Arrived at noon	
			Weather Rained all day.	

Army Form C. 2118

WAR DIARY
or
INTELLIGENCE SUMMARY
(Erase heading not required.)

Instructions regarding War Diaries and Intelligence Summaries are contained in F. S. Regs., Part II. and the Staff Manual respectively. Title Pages will be prepared in manuscript.

Place	Date	Hour	Summary of Events and Information	Remarks and references to Appendices
Mametz	5/12/15		Billetted in Mametz.	
			Weather fair.	

Army Form C. 2118

WAR DIARY
or
INTELLIGENCE SUMMARY
(Erase heading not required.)

Instructions regarding War Diaries and Intelligence Summaries are contained in F. S. Regs., Part II. and the Staff Manual respectively. Title Pages will be prepared in manuscript.

Place	Date	Hour	Summary of Events and Information	Remarks and references to Appendices
Mametz	6/12/15	4.00am	124th Fd. Co. R.E. arrived in Mametz & billetted in the area west of 123rd Fd Co R.E. billets. Company engaged in repacking carts and wagons all day.	
		3.0pm	151st Fd Co R.E. arrived bringing Sapper F. Harris 123rd Co. with them. This completed our establishment	

Weather Morning Fair
Afternoon Rain

1875 Wt. W593/826 1,000,000 4/15 J.B.C. & A. A.D.S.S./Forms/C. 2118.

Army Form C. 2118

WAR DIARY
or
INTELLIGENCE SUMMARY
(Erase heading not required.)

Instructions regarding War Diaries and Intelligence Summaries are contained in F. S. Regs., Part II. and the Staff Manual respectively. Title Pages will be prepared in manuscript.

Place	Date	Hour	Summary of Events and Information	Remarks and references to Appendices
Mametz	7/1/15		Company engaged all day in examination & inspection of stores & equipment.	
			Weather Dull & wet	

1875 Wt. W593/826 1,000,000 4/15 J.B.C. & A. A.D.S.S./Forms/C. 2118.

Army Form C. 2118

WAR DIARY
or
INTELLIGENCE SUMMARY
(Erase heading not required.)

Instructions regarding War Diaries and Intelligence Summaries are contained in F. S. Regs., Part II. and the Staff Manual respectively. Title Pages will be prepared in manuscript.

Place	Date	Hour	Summary of Events and Information	Remarks and references to Appendices
Mametz	8/12/15	9 a.m.	Received orders from C.R.E. to report to G.O.C. 113th Brigade.	
		1:00 pm	Did so & received orders to instruct infantry of 113th Brigade in Engineering work viz, wire obstacles, Breastworks, Splinter Proof Shelters, construction of Communication trenches etc.	
		6:00 pm	Stores for above arrived at Mametz	

Weather Showery

J.D.

WAR DIARY
or
INTELLIGENCE SUMMARY
(Erase heading not required.)

Army Form C. 2118

Place	Date	Hour	Summary of Events and Information	Remarks and references to Appendices
Merville	9/10/15	2.00am.	Received orders from C.R.E. 38th Div. that the Company will be attached to the Guards Division on the 10th inst. Transport to be left behind with exception of cooks vehicle & vehicle for entrenching tools. Orders as to time of leaving to be sent later.	
		6.30pm	Received orders from Headquarters 38th Division that the Company less Transport detailed above will proceed tomorrow to ST. VENANT, and be billetted there for the night under arrangements to be made by the 46th Division and on the following day will proceed to LAVENTIE and be attached to the Guards Division for instruction	
		7.00pm	Received the same orders as above from C.R.E. 38th Division.	

Weather Exceedingly wet & cold.

J.W.A.

Army Form C. 2118

WAR DIARY
or
INTELLIGENCE SUMMARY
(Erase heading not required.)

Instructions regarding War Diaries and Intelligence Summaries are contained in F. S. Regs., Part II. and the Staff Manual respectively. Title Pages will be prepared in manuscript.

Place	Date	Hour	Summary of Events and Information	Remarks and references to Appendices
Manetz	10/11/15	8.30am	Company paraded less Transport detailed in yesterdays diary at 8-30am. and marched to ST. VENANT. Strength 5 officers 185 N.C.O.'s & men and 35 horses.	
		1.00pm	Arrived S.T. VENANT and billetted in two adjoining farmhouses south of the town	
			Weather Rained in morning, dry in afternoon	

1875 Wt. W593/826 1,000,000 4/15 J.B.C. & A. A.D.S.S./Forms/C. 2118.

Army Form C. 2118

WAR DIARY
or
INTELLIGENCE SUMMARY

(Erase heading not required.)

Instructions regarding War Diaries and Intelligence Summaries are contained in F. S. Regs., Part II. and the Staff Manual respectively. Title Pages will be prepared in manuscript.

Place	Date	Hour	Summary of Events and Information	Remarks and references to Appendices
Laventie	11/12/15	8·00 a.m.	Paraded and marched to Laventie (about 11 miles) Billetted in village alongside 55th, 75th and 76th Field Coys. R.E. No 1 Section attached to 75th Field Co. for work and instruction. Nos 2 and 4 Sections to 55th Field Co. and No 3 Section to 76th Field Co. —	
			Weather. Rained practically all day	

MK

Army Form C. 2118

WAR DIARY
or
INTELLIGENCE SUMMARY
(Erase heading not required.)

Place	Date	Hour	Summary of Events and Information	Remarks and references to Appendices
Laventie	15.12.15		All sections at work under the O/C's. Held C.O. Guards Division. Personally visited northern quarter of line held by Guards Division. Engineers work mainly drainage. Country very flat. Great difficulty in getting water away. In this part it is impossible to dig trenches owing to the water. The firing line is a continuous breastwork. No 1 Section employed on Drainage. No 2 " " " Railway Repair. No 3 " " " construction of Point d'appui. No 4 " " " Drainage. Weather fair in morning. Showers in afternoon.	JHB.

Army Form C. 21

WAR DIARY
or
INTELLIGENCE SUMMARY
(Erase heading not required.)

Instructions regarding War Diaries and Intelligence Summaries are contained in F. S. Regs., Part II. and the Staff Manual respectively. Title Pages will be prepared in manuscript.

Place	Date	Hour	Summary of Events and Information	Remarks and references to Appendices
Laventie	13/11/15		Sections employed on same work as yesterday only No 1 on Revetting instead. Obtained rubber boots for men working in water.	
			Weather fine showery	JnL

1875 Wt. W593/826 1,000,000 4/15 J.B.C. & A. A.D.S.S./Forms/C. 2118.

Army Form C. 2118

WAR DIARY
or
INTELLIGENCE SUMMARY
(Erase heading not required.)

Instructions regarding War Diaries and Intelligence Summaries are contained in F. S. Regs., Part II. and the Staff Manual respectively. Title Pages will be prepared in manuscript.

Place	Date	Hour	Summary of Events and Information	Remarks and references to Appendices
Laventie	14.12.15		Sections not employed on drainage. Other sections as before. Personally visited trenches — Heavy shelling on both sides. Drainage easier.	
			Weather Hard frost.	

J.M.

Army Form C. 2118.

WAR DIARY
or
INTELLIGENCE SUMMARY
(Erase heading not required.)

Instructions regarding War Diaries and Intelligence Summaries are contained in F.S. Regs., Part II. and the Staff Manual respectively. Title Pages will be prepared in manuscript.

Place	Date	Hour	Summary of Events and Information	Remarks and references to Appendices
Bapaume	15.12.16		Sections at work as follows.	
			No 1 Revetting	
			No 2 Railway repairs	
			No 3 Revetting	
			No 4 Constructing Point d'appui	
			Weather. Cold.	

Army Form C. 2118

WAR DIARY
or
INTELLIGENCE SUMMARY

(Erase heading not required.)

Instructions regarding War Diaries and Intelligence Summaries are contained in F. S. Regs., Part II. and the Staff Manual respectively. Title Pages will be prepared in manuscript.

Place	Date	Hour	Summary of Events and Information	Remarks and references to Appendices
Lavantie	16.12.15		Sections at work as follows.	
			No 1 Making platforms for gas cylinders	
			No 2 Railway Repairs	
			No 3 Revetting	
			No 4 Constructing strong point	
			Personally visited northern section.	
			Weather. Showery.	
			JH.	

1875 Wt. W593/826 1,000,000 4/15 J.B.C. & A. A.D.S.S./Forms/C. 2118.

Army Form C. 2118

WAR DIARY
or
INTELLIGENCE SUMMARY
(Erase heading not required.)

Place	Date	Hour	Summary of Events and Information	Remarks and references to Appendices
Laventie	17.12.15		Sections at work as follows:-	
			No. 1 Drainage	
			No. 2 Railway Repairs & Night work.	
			No. 3 Revetting	
			No. 4 Constructing Point d'appui.	
			Personally visited southern section down to Neuve Chapelle village.	
			Weather Showery.	
			J.H.L.	

Army Form C. 2118

WAR DIARY or INTELLIGENCE SUMMARY

(Erase heading not required.)

Instructions regarding War Diaries and Intelligence Summaries are contained in F. S. Regs., Part II. and the Staff Manual respectively. Title Pages will be prepared in manuscript.

Place	Date	Hour	Summary of Events and Information	Remarks and references to Appendices
LAVENTIE	18·12·15		Sections at work as follows.	
			No 1. Drainage	
			No 2. Repairs to Railway & Drainage	
			No 3. Revetting Communication trench with hurdles.	
			No 4. Constructing points d'appui.	
			Nos 1, 2, and 3 sections were working at night.	
			All men of the company were given baths and clean underclothing at the Corps baths	
			weather dry	

J.L.

Army Form C. 2118

WAR DIARY
or
INTELLIGENCE SUMMARY

(Erase heading not required.)

Place	Date	Hour	Summary of Events and Information	Remarks and references to Appendices
LAVENTIE.	19.12.15	10 a.m.	Received instructions by telegram from Headquarters 38th Division to proceed to billets near MERVILLE in square K.28.	
		9.0 a.m.	Marched off and arrived in billetting area at 1.0 p.m. The Interpreter and a Corporal from the Company details at MAMETZ had arrived the previous night and had arranged the billets in K.28. At 3.0 p.m. the 13th Bn. R.W.F. arrived with instructions to billet in the same area. This being impossible they had to move further west to LE SART.	
		9.0 p.m.	Received instructions from 113th Brigade Headquarters to change billets to LE SART village and to farm houses on Hazebrouck Road at point in K.22.d.2.3.	

Weather fair

Army Form C. 2118

WAR DIARY
or
INTELLIGENCE SUMMARY

(Erase heading not required.)

Instructions regarding War Diaries and Intelligence Summaries are contained in F. S. Regs., Part II. and the Staff Manual respectively. Title Pages will be prepared in manuscript.

Place	Date	Hour	Summary of Events and Information	Remarks and references to Appendices
LE SART.	20/12/15.	12 noon	Changed billets as instructed yesterday -	
		3.30 pm	Details from MAMETZ arrived under the command of LIEUT. L. W. ATKINSON. R.E.	
			weather fair	

Army Form C. 2118

WAR DIARY
~~INTELLIGENCE SUMMARY~~
(Erase heading not required.)

Place	Date	Hour	Summary of Events and Information	Remarks and references to Appendices
LE SART.	31.12.15		No 3 Section at work repairing billets K.33 a.3.3. No 1 Section preparing rifle range for 113th Bde. at point K.20.C.3.8. Personally reported to C.R.E. 38th Division at ~~####~~ ST. VENANT. Weather Showery all day	

J. Lawrence

Army Form C. 2118

WAR DIARY
or
INTELLIGENCE SUMMARY
(Erase heading not required.)

Instructions regarding War Diaries and Intelligence Summaries are contained in F. S. Regs., Part II. and the Staff Manual respectively. Title Pages will be prepared in manuscript.

Place	Date	Hour	Summary of Events and Information	Remarks and references to Appendices
LE SART.	22/12/15		No 1 section at work preparing 30 yard Rifle Range near 113th Bde Headquarters. No 3 Section completed repairs to R.F.A. billet. Personally arranged with G.O.C. 113th Bde. a scheme for training the Infantry in Field Engineer Scheme as follows. The R.E. will put 64 officers NCOs & men per battalion through a one days course in sandbag work, revetting, constructing obstacles, dugouts etc. These men will then train the remainder of their battalions under the supervision of the R.E. Weather Fair.	

Army Form C. 2118

WAR DIARY
or
INTELLIGENCE SUMMARY

(Erase heading not required.)

Place	Date	Hour	Summary of Events and Information	Remarks and references to Appendices
LE SART.	25/12/15		Consulted G.O.C. 114th Bde. on the training of his Brigade in Field Engineering. Arranged a similar course to that for the 113th Bde. Lieut. W. ATKINSON. proceeded to LACOUTRIE to be attached to the 151st Field Co. R.E. for 3 days instruction in the trenches. LIEUT. RICHARDS AND 30 MEN. proceeded to ST. VENANT for work under C.R.E. Weather very wet.	

Army Form C. 2118

WAR DIARY
or
INTELLIGENCE SUMMARY

(Erase heading not required.)

Instructions regarding War Diaries and Intelligence Summaries are contained in F. S. Regs., Part II. and the Staff Manual respectively. Title Pages will be prepared in manuscript.

Place	Date	Hour	Summary of Events and Information	Remarks and references to Appendices
LE SART.	24/10/15	—	LIEUT FREETH and NCO's instructed 128 Officers NCO's men of 13th & 16th Bns R.W.F. in Field Engineering. No 1 Section building rifle range. # Weather bad.	

Army Form C. 2118

WAR DIARY
or
INTELLIGENCE SUMMARY.
(Erase heading not required.)

Instructions regarding War Diaries and Intelligence Summaries are contained in F. S. Regs., Part II and the Staff Manual respectively. Title pages will be prepared in manuscript.

Place	Date	Hour	Summary of Events and Information	Remarks and references to Appendices
LE SART.	25/12/15		Christmas Day. Holiday for all men.	
			weather fair	

Army Form C. 2118

WAR DIARY
or
INTELLIGENCE SUMMARY.
(Erase heading not required.)

Instructions regarding War Diaries and Intelligence Summaries are contained in F. S. Regs., Part II. and the Staff Manual respectively. Title pages will be prepared in manuscript.

Place	Date	Hour	Summary of Events and Information	Remarks and references to Appendices
LE SART.	30/10/15		No WORK.	
			"Weather fair"	

J.S.

#353 Wt. W2544/1454 700,000 5/15 D. D. & L. A.D.S.S./Forms/C. 2118.

Army Form C. 2118

WAR DIARY
or
INTELLIGENCE SUMMARY.
(Erase heading not required.)

Instructions regarding War Diaries and Intelligence Summaries are contained in F. S. Regs., Part II. and the Staff Manual respectively. Title pages will be prepared in manuscript.

Place	Date	Hour	Summary of Events and Information	Remarks and references to Appendices
LE SART.	27.12.15		LIEUT. McLEAN and 20 men left at 3 p.m. for Corps Artillery Headquarters to work on artillery observation posts.	
			LIEUT SOUTER started instruction of Infantry of 114th Bde in Field Engineering.	
			MAJOR I.W. LAMONBY PRESIDENT of F.G. Court Marshall at 38th Div Amm. Sub. Park.	
			Weather Fine	

Army Form C. 2118

WAR DIARY
or
INTELLIGENCE SUMMARY.
(Erase heading not required.)

Instructions regarding War Diaries and Intelligence Summaries are contained in F. S. Regs., Part II. and the Staff Manual respectively. Title pages will be prepared in manuscript.

Place	Date	Hour	Summary of Events and Information	Remarks and references to Appendices
LE SART	28.12.15		Company instructing 113th & 114th Bdes. in Field Engineering. Weather fine.	

Army Form C. 2118

WAR DIARY
or
INTELLIGENCE SUMMARY.
(Erase heading not required.)

Instructions regarding War Diaries and Intelligence Summaries are contained in F. S. Regs., Part II. and the Staff Manual respectively. Title pages will be prepared in manuscript.

Place	Date	Hour	Summary of Events and Information	Remarks and references to Appendices
LE SART	29/10/15		Company instructing 113th & 114th Coles. in Field Engineering Weather Fine	

Smg.

Army Form C. 2118.

WAR DIARY
or
INTELLIGENCE SUMMARY.
(Erase heading not required.)

Instructions regarding War Diaries and Intelligence Summaries are contained in F. S. Regs., Part II. and the Staff Manual respectively. Title pages will be prepared in manuscript.

Place	Date	Hour	Summary of Events and Information	Remarks and references to Appendices
LE SART.	30/10/15		Instruction of 113th & 114th Bdes. in Field Engineering carried out by men of the Company. Reported to S.O.C. 113th Bde. on Horse Standings. Weather Fine	

Army Form C. 2118

WAR DIARY
or
INTELLIGENCE SUMMARY.

(Erase heading not required.)

Instructions regarding War Diaries and Intelligence Summaries are contained in F. S. Regs., Part II. and the Staff Manual respectively. Title pages will be prepared in manuscript.

Place	Date	Hour	Summary of Events and Information	Remarks and references to Appendices
LESART	31/10/15		Instruction of 113th & 114th Bdes in Field Engineering carried out as before.	

$353 Wt. W3544/1454 700,000 5/15 D. D. & L. A.D.S.S./Forms/C. 2118.

123rd F.C.R.E.
Vol. 2

38

Army Form C. 2118.

WAR DIARY
or
INTELLIGENCE SUMMARY.
(Erase heading not required.)

Instructions regarding War Diaries and Intelligence Summaries are contained in F.S. Regs., Part II. and the Staff Manual respectively. Title pages will be prepared in manuscript.

Place	Date	Hour	Summary of Events and Information	Remarks and references to Appendices
LE SART.	1.1.16.		Instruction of 114th Bde. in Field Engineering completed. 113th Bde. instruction carried out as usual.	
			Weather Fine.	

Army Form C. 2118.

WAR DIARY
or
INTELLIGENCE SUMMARY.
(Erase heading not required.)

Place	Date	Hour	Summary of Events and Information	Remarks and references to Appendices
LE SART.	2.1.16		Instruction of 113th Bde completed.	
			Weather Very wet.	

Army Form C. 2118.

WAR DIARY
or
INTELLIGENCE SUMMARY.
(Erase heading not required.)

Instructions regarding War Diaries and Intelligence Summaries are contained in F. S. Regs., Part II. and the Staff Manual respectively. Title pages will be prepared in manuscript.

Place	Date	Hour	Summary of Events and Information	Remarks and references to Appendices
LE SART.	3.1.16.		Company on training - Grenade throwing, Demolition, & Blocks & Tackles.	
			Weather Fine.	

Army Form C. 2118.

WAR DIARY
or
INTELLIGENCE SUMMARY.
(Erase heading not required.)

Instructions regarding War Diaries and Intelligence Summaries are contained in F. S. Regs., Part II. and the Staff Manual respectively. Title pages will be prepared in manuscript.

Place	Date	Hour	Summary of Events and Information	Remarks and references to Appendices
LE SART	4·1·16		Company on Training Grenades, Demolition Blocks & Tackles. MAJOR I. W. LAMONBY left to go round 19th DIVISION area. Weather Fine	

Army Form C. 2118.

WAR DIARY
or
INTELLIGENCE SUMMARY.
(Erase heading not required.)

Instructions regarding War Diaries and Intelligence Summaries are contained in F. S. Regs., Part II and the Staff Manual respectively. Title pages will be prepared in manuscript.

Place	Date	Hour	Summary of Events and Information	Remarks and references to Appendices
LE SART.	5.1.16.		Company training on Grenade work Demolition and Blocks & Tackles. Weather fine	J.L.

2353 Wt. W2544/1454 700,000 5/15 D.D.&L. A.D.S.S./Forms/C. 2118.

WAR DIARY or INTELLIGENCE SUMMARY

Army Form C. 2118

Place	Date	Hour	Summary of Events and Information	Remarks and references to Appendices
LE SART.	6.1.16		Company on training. Demolition. Range practice 30 rounds per man. Blocks & Tackle. MAJOR I.W. LAMONBY returned from LACOUTRE. Weather Fine	

Army Form C. 2118

WAR DIARY
or
INTELLIGENCE SUMMARY

(Erase heading not required.)

Instructions regarding War Diaries and Intelligence Summaries are contained in F. S. Regs., Part II. and the Staff Manual respectively. Title Pages will be prepared in manuscript.

Place	Date	Hour	Summary of Events and Information	Remarks and references to Appendices
LE SART.	7.1.16.		Company training as yesterday	
			Weather Fine	

JM.

Army Form C. 2118

WAR DIARY
or
INTELLIGENCE SUMMARY

(Erase heading not required.)

Instructions regarding War Diaries and Intelligence Summaries are contained in F. S. Regs., Part II. and the Staff Manual respectively. Title Pages will be prepared in manuscript.

Place	Date	Hour	Summary of Events and Information	Remarks and references to Appendices
LE SART	8.1.16		Company training in demolition & bomb throwing	

1875 Wt. W593/826 1,000,000 4/15 J.B.C. & A. A.D.S.S./Forms/C. 2118.

Army Form C. 2118

WAR DIARY
or
INTELLIGENCE SUMMARY
(Erase heading not required.)

Place	Date	Hour	Summary of Events and Information	Remarks and references to Appendices
Le Sart	9/1/16		Nil	

Army Form C. 2118

WAR DIARY
or
INTELLIGENCE SUMMARY

(Erase heading not required.)

Instructions regarding War Diaries and Intelligence Summaries are contained in F. S. Regs., Part II. and the Staff Manual respectively. Title Pages will be prepared in manuscript.

Place	Date	Hour	Summary of Events and Information	Remarks and references to Appendices
Le Sart	10/4/16		Packing tool carts. Received orders to move company to Lacouture tomorrow to 113th Bde. in front line to be attached. Weather fine. JMcT	

Army Form C. 2118

WAR DIARY
or
INTELLIGENCE SUMMARY
(Erase heading not required.)

Instructions regarding War Diaries and Intelligence Summaries are contained in F. S. Regs., Part II. and the Staff Manual respectively. Title Pages will be prepared in manuscript.

Place	Date	Hour	Summary of Events and Information	Remarks and references to Appendices
Le Sart	10/1/16		Left Le Sart 8 am & arrived at billets at R 34 d 3, 2, at 12 noon. Took over line from S, 10, c, 7, 5 to S 21 d 8, 3. Sheet 36 B. Details of Nos 1 and 4 Sections formed into Details Section under Coy Sergt Major Evans. Weather fine	

Place	Date	Hour	Summary of Events and Information	Remarks and references to Appendices
Laventie	12/1/16		No 2 Section with 2ND LIEUT. A. F. SOUTAR took over line from Farm Corner to Cope Street, No 3 Section under LIEUT FREETH took over line from Farm Corner to Buvuque Rue. Details Section at work on Rope Keep.	

WAR DIARY
or
INTELLIGENCE SUMMARY

(Erase heading not required.)

Army Form C. 2118

Place	Date	Hour	Summary of Events and Information	Remarks and references to Appendices
Facentill	13/1/16		All sections at work on front line. Infantry working parties detailed to sections as follows	
			Nº 2 — 57 men	
			Nº 3 — 60 men	
			Details — 50 men	

JWL.

Army Form C. 2118

WAR DIARY
or
INTELLIGENCE SUMMARY
(Erase heading not required.)

Instructions regarding War Diaries and Intelligence Summaries are contained in F. S. Regs., Part II. and the Staff Manual respectively. Title Pages will be prepared in manuscript.

Place	Date	Hour	Summary of Events and Information	Remarks and references to Appendices
Lacouture	14/1/16		8 men at work from Cope Street to Bond Street in N° Section area during the day. Owing to infantry reliefs no infantry working parties were available during the night. R E at work on dugouts + on technical work.	

Int.

Army Form C. 2118

WAR DIARY
or
INTELLIGENCE SUMMARY
(Erase heading not required.)

Instructions regarding War Diaries and Intelligence Summaries are contained in F. S. Regs., Part II. and the Staff Manual respectively. Title Pages will be prepared in manuscript.

Place	Date	Hour	Summary of Events and Information	Remarks and references to Appendices
Lacouture	15/1/16		Working parties as follows with sections. 79 with No 2 Section 50 with No 3 & 50 with Details.	
			No 2 Section working party short 9 men, 100 had been promised works laid out accordingly	
			JM.	

1875 Wt. W593/826 1,000,000 4/15 J.B.C. & A. A.D.S.S./Forms/C. 2118.

Army Form C. 2118

WAR DIARY
or
INTELLIGENCE SUMMARY

(Erase heading not required.)

Place	Date	Hour	Summary of Events and Information	Remarks and references to Appendices
Lacouture	16/1/16		Infantry working parties 50 men with Details & 50 with No 2 Section. None turned up for No 3. All men on No 2 Section area to be concentrated on No 6 & 7 Posts to complete these	

Army Form C. 2118

WAR DIARY
or
INTELLIGENCE SUMMARY
(Erase heading not required.)

Instructions regarding War Diaries and Intelligence Summaries are contained in F. S. Regs., Part II. and the Staff Manual respectively. Title Pages will be prepared in manuscript.

Place	Date	Hour	Summary of Events and Information	Remarks and references to Appendices
Lacouture	17/1/16		Working parties with Sections No 2 100 men No 3 50 " Details 50 " Work at farm corner & No 6 posts progressing fairly well. 62460 Second Corp. St Jago slightly wounded in right arm.	
Lacouture	18/1/16		Sections on night work. Farm Corner traverses set out.	
do	19/1/16		Sections worked as usual. Progress made on front line improvements.	
do	20/1/16		Work as usual. Machine gun emplacement started near Cadbury Street.	

WAR DIARY
or
INTELLIGENCE SUMMARY

(Erase heading not required.)

Army Form C. 2118

Instructions regarding War Diaries and Intelligence Summaries are contained in F. S. Regs., Part II. and the Staff Manual respectively. Title Pages will be prepared in manuscript.

Place	Date	Hour	Summary of Events and Information	Remarks and references to Appendices
Lacouture	21/1/16		Sections at work as usual. Infantry working parties were not at all energetic. New dugout completed at Farm Corner. LIEUT M^cLEAN and party of 20 men who had been building observation posts for the 25th Bde R.G.A. returned to the Company. JMT.	
do.	22/1/16		Took over Right Sector of 19th Divisional area from N° 82nd Field Co. Work as usual. JMT	
Locontine	23/1/16		The R.E. work. Infantry working parties employed in carrying down stores to the front line. JMT	
do.	24/1/16		LIEUT RICHARDS and 35 men who had been attached to the C.R.E. 38th Div returned to the Company. The 124th Field Co R.E. took over line from QUINQUE RUE to N° 5 POST. THIS COMPANY took over line from S.16.A.0.1½. to Mule Street inclusive. The company moved billets to X.5.C.9.5. JMT.	

Army Form C. 2118

WAR DIARY
or
INTELLIGENCE SUMMARY
(Erase heading not required.)

Instructions regarding War Diaries and Intelligence Summaries are contained in F. S. Regs., Part II and the Staff Manual respectively. Title Pages will be prepared in manuscript.

Place	Date	Hour	Summary of Events and Information	Remarks and references to Appendices
Laventie	25/1/16		10810 O. Corporal W. G. Lloyd slightly wounded in right leg. Sappers at work on front line with infantry working parties. gnt.	
do.	26/1/16		Work carried on as usual and on new drain running S.E. from Factory Corner. gnt.	
do.	27/1/16		Work as usual on front line. gnt.	
do.	28/1/16		Arrangements made with garrison in front line for 96 men to be detailed as working parties for improvement of front line. Good progress made at Boars Head. gnt.	
do.	29/1/16		Working parties as usual.	
do.	30/1/16		Infantry working parties doing day work instead of night work. gnt.	

Army Form C. 2118

WAR DIARY
or
INTELLIGENCE SUMMARY
(Erase heading not required.)

Instructions regarding War Diaries and Intelligence Summaries are contained in F. S. Regs., Part II. and the Staff Manual respectively. Title Pages will be prepared in manuscript.

Place	Date	Hour	Summary of Events and Information	Remarks and references to Appendices
Lacouture	31/1/16		R.E. at work as usual. No infantry parties available as battalions were relieving.	

A.G's. Office.
   BASE.

    Enclosed please find War Diary for this Company for the Month of February, ultimo.

                         Major R.E.
               O.C. 123rd Field Co.R.E

B.E.F.
  1.3.16.

Army Form C. 2118

WAR DIARY
or
INTELLIGENCE SUMMARY
(Erase heading not required.)

Place	Date	Hour	Summary of Events and Information	Remarks and references to Appendices
Lacouture	1/2/16		Work as usual on front line. JnL.	
	2/2/16		do. New post started to the right of Cockspur Street on old Rangers trench. LIEUT. T.C. FREETH slightly wounded in right leg. JnL.	
	3/2/16		work as usual JnL.	
	4/2/16		do.	
	5/2/16		do.	
	6/2/16		do.	
	7/2/16		do.	
	8/2/16		Brigade relief 114th Brigade took over line from 113th Bde. Company had a holiday. JnL.	

Army Form C. 2118

WAR DIARY
or
INTELLIGENCE SUMMARY
(Erase heading not required.)

Instructions regarding War Diaries and Intelligence Summaries are contained in F. S. Regs., Part II and the Staff Manual respectively. Title Pages will be prepared in manuscript.

Place	Date	Hour	Summary of Events and Information	Remarks and references to Appendices
Facextere	9/7/16		Work continued on Rangers Trench & on Bond + Cookafern Communication Trenches 2.LIEUT. W.A. EVANS joined the Company for duty.	
	10/7/16		do.	
	11/7/16		do.	
	12/7/16		do.	
	13/7/16		do.	
	14/7/16		do. Inspection of Festubert area at present worked by East Anglian Field Co RE made. Orders received to move to billets at LE TOURET on 17th inst.	
	15/7/16		do. do.	
	16/7/16		Area at present being worked handed over to 124th Field GRE	
	17/7/16		Company moved to billets at LE TOURET Map Reference X.15.d.8.3.	

1875 Wt. W593/826 1,000,000 4/15 J.B.C. & A. A.D.S.S./Forms/C. 2118.

Army Form C. 2118

WAR DIARY
or
INTELLIGENCE SUMMARY

(Erase heading not required.)

Instructions regarding War Diaries and Intelligence Summaries are contained in F.S. Regs., Part II. and the Staff Manual respectively. Title Pages will be prepared in manuscript.

Place	Date	Hour	Summary of Events and Information	Remarks and references to Appendices
LE TOURET	18/9/16		Officers & NCO's inspecting works & trenches.	
	19/9/16		do.	
	20/9/16		38th Division took over Leturbet area, work started on reclaiming Old British Line.	
	21/9/16		Work continued on reclaiming Old British Line, construction of dugouts, machine gun emplacements, drainage, etc.	
	22/9/16		do.	
	23/9/16		do.	
	24/9/16		do.	
	25/9/16		do.	
	26/9/16		do.	
	27/9/16		do.	
	28/9/16		do. Work started on joining up ISLANDS or front line.	
	29/9/16		do.	

Signed, Major R.E.

1875 Wt. W593/826 1,000,000 4/15 J.B.C. & A. A.D.S.S./Forms/C. 2118.

Thos. De La Rue & Co. Ltd., Bunhill Row, E.C.
W3125/1706 1,200m 6/15

Forms C. 348 / 61

Army Form C. 348.

No. *Secret?*

MEMORANDUM.

From O.C.
      123rd Field Co. R.E.

To D.A.G.,
      3rd Echelon,
      BASE.

From

To

ANSWER.

3. 4. 1916

_____ 191

Enclosed please find War Diary for this Company for the month of March ultimo.

J. Howells
Lieut R.E.
for O.C. 123rd Field Co. R.E

Army Form C. 2118

WAR DIARY
or
INTELLIGENCE SUMMARY
(Erase heading not required.)

Instructions regarding War Diaries and Intelligence Summaries are contained in F. S. Regs., Part II. and the Staff Manual respectively. Title Pages will be prepared in manuscript.

Place	Date	Hour	Summary of Events and Information	Remarks and references to Appendices
Le Touret X.15.d.6.2.	1/3/16		Work continued in reclaiming OBL (old Portuguese line) construction of ordinary dugouts, concrete machine gun emplacements, drainage of connecting up isolated sections of connecting trenches. Opening up old mined and existing tramways:- Also OPs	
	2/3/16		do do do do do	
	3/3/16		do do do do do	
	4/3/16		2nd Lieut A.L. Carroll joined. Work as above continued. One Section of the 204th F Coy R.E. which had been attached for instruction left.	
	5/3/16		Work as above continued. Sapper H. Thorncombe wounded by bullet.	
	6/3/16		Work as above continued.	
	7/3/16		Work as above continued. Remainder of 204th F Coy R.E. left.	
	8/3/16		Work as above continued	
	9/3/16		Work as above continued	
	10/3/16		Work as above continued	
	11/3/16		Work as above continued	

Army Form C. 2118

WAR DIARY
or
INTELLIGENCE SUMMARY
(Erase heading not required.)

Instructions regarding War Diaries and Intelligence Summaries are contained in F.S. Regs., Part II. and the Staff Manual respectively. Title Pages will be prepared in manuscript.

Place	Date	Hour	Summary of Events and Information	Remarks and references to Appendices
Le Touret X.15.d.82.	12/3/16		Work carried on reclaiming old British line. Construction of dugouts, concrete Machine gun emplacements O.P.s. Connecting up Kendo extension of Communication Trenches Opening up old mine catching Tramway & levelling village line. Lieut Atkinson wounded by Shrapnel.	
"	13/3/16		Work continued as above. 2nd Lieut A.P. Carroll transferred to 151 st of Coy.	
"	14/3/16		Lieut Donnelli joined. Worked continued as above	
	15/3/16		Work Continued as above.	
	16/3/16		Work Continued as above	
	17/3/16		Work Continued as above	
	18/3/16		Work Continued as above. 2nd Lieut J.S. Lethbridge joined the Company from Base Power.	
	19/3/16		Work continued as above. Dap ditch in Canadian orchard drained into German lines. freeing our own Trenches of water	
	20/3/16		Work as above	
	21/3/16		do	
	22/3/16		do	
	23/3/16		do	

Army Form C. 2118

WAR DIARY
or
INTELLIGENCE SUMMARY
(Erase heading not required.)

Instructions regarding War Diaries and Intelligence Summaries are contained in F. S. Regs., Part II. and the Staff Manual respectively. Title Pages will be prepared in manuscript.

Place	Date	Hour	Summary of Events and Information	Remarks and references to Appendices
Le Touret X.15.d.8.2.	24/3/16		Major J. W. Lamonby RE left to be Acting C.R.E. 36th Division during CRE's absence on leave. Lieut. J. Howells assumed command of Company.	
	25/3/16		Work continued as above	
	26/3/16		do.	
	27/3/16		do.	
	28/3/16		do.	
	29/3/16		do.	
	30/3/16		do. Weather improving - work progressing very well on Festubert line to drying up of the land.	
	31/3/16		Section the operations during the month.	

Army Form C. 348.

MEMORANDUM.

From O.C.
123rd FIELD COMPANY
ROYAL ENGINEERS.

To Officer
i/c. A.G's Office
Base

3. 5. 1916

Enclosed please find War
Diary of this Company
for month of April, ultimo.

T. C. Freeth
Lieut R.E.
for O.C. 123rd FIELD COMPANY
ROYAL ENGINEERS.

123 F.C.R.E.
Vol. 5.

WAR DIARY
or
INTELLIGENCE SUMMARY

(Erase heading not required.)

Army Form C. 2118

Place	Date	Hour	Summary of Events and Information	Remarks and references to Appendices
Le Touret X.15.d.8.2	1/4/16		Work continued in reclaiming Old British lines, construction of dugouts, Concrete Machine Gun emplacements, OPs. Connecting up islands on Front line. Extension of communication trenches. Wiring village line, maintaining water service, installing new pipe line from artesian well at Le Plantin.	
"	2/4/16		Work continued as above	
"	3/4/16		Work continued as above	
"	4/4/16		Work continued as above. Lieut Evans entered Hospital Illness.	
"	5/4/16		Work continued as above	
	6/4/16		Work continued as above	
	7/4/16		Work continued as above. 8 Reinforcements arrived from Base	
	9/4/16		Work continued as above.	
	10/4/16		Work continued as above.	

123rd FIELD COMPANY
ROYAL ENGINEERS.

WAR DIARY or INTELLIGENCE SUMMARY

Army Form C. 2118

Place	Date	Hour	Summary of Events and Information	Remarks and references to Appendices
Le Touret S.15a.8.2	11/4/16		Work continued on reclaiming old British line. Construction of dugouts, machine gun emplacements, O.P.s connecting up islands in front line. Between existing communication trenches, opening up old ones. Extending tramline, wiring village line, maintaining existing pipe line. Extending tramline, new pipe line to front line from Le Plantin.	
	12/4/16		Work continued as above. Sapper W. Dare wounded by billet & died afterwards.	
	13/4/16		Work continued as above.	
	14/4/16		Work continued as above. The defence of Canadian trenches virtually restored.	
	15/4/16		Preparing to move awaiting instructions. Left Le Touret for Estaires. Marched there and billeted in Estaires.	
Estaires	16/4/16		Left Estaires for R.12.c.6.5. 284 F.Coy. returned to their units. Weather very wet.	
R.12.c.6.5	17/4/16		Left Estaires for R.12.c.6.5. remained at R.12.c.6.5. for the night and proceeded to M.9.b.6.9. Levantie. Weather very wet. Major Lewendy returned and took over command.	✓
Levantie M.9.b.6.9	18/4/16		Company cleaned billets.	

123rd FIELD COMPANY
ROYAL ENGINEERS.

WAR DIARY or INTELLIGENCE SUMMARY

Army Form C. 2118

Place	Date	Hour	Summary of Events and Information	Remarks and references to Appendices
Loomtie M.9.8.69	19/4/16		Company HQ Officers & NCOs went over new area to take over work from the 81st F. Coy. General improvement of billets taken in hand.	
"	20/4/16		Construction of New Rifle Butt Head Rests' and Left Batt Head Rests continued. Construction of N.& Emp. continued on Front line. Wiring around Keeps.	
"	21/4/16		Work continued as above.	
"	22/4/16		Work continued as above. A scheme was initiated from the reclamation of the reserve line. Weather very bad. Sapping started to Crater opposite Colwin Street	
"	23/4/16		Work continued as above.	
"	24/4/16		Work continued as above, but generally concentrated on New Reserve line. Lieut Harper & 19 Batt. Pioneers attached to unit.	
"	25/4/16		Work continued as above. Weather improved considerably	
"	26/4/16		Work continued as above. Weather very fine & warm	
"	27/4/16		Work continued as above. "	
"	28/4/16		Work continued as above. Seeing Beautiful roads started. Major Lowenberg proceeded to England on leave. Lt Howells acting O.C.	Transfer to the hospital during this days by passing Bull Toe.
"	29/4/16		Work continued as above. Sapper T.J. Davis wounded by bullet.	
"	30/4/16		Work continued as above. Lieut Leeth arrived from Base and took over command	

128th FIELD COMPANY
ROYAL ENGINEERS.

WAR DIARY
or
INTELLIGENCE SUMMARY
(Erase heading not required.)

Army Form C. 2118

XXXVIII

123 F.C. R.E.

Place	Date	Hour	Summary of Events and Information	Remarks and references to Appendices
LAVENTIE	1/5/16		Work continued on reclaiming old reserve line principally of work Construction of Right and Left of new Boter Hope continued. Wiring of keeps continued. New Colvin enp commenced to left centre of mine areaeft. Scheme of making gun emplacement of Rifle Ranges of Storm up. initiated. Screening roads. Improvements to communication trenches. Maintenance of tramlines.	
	2/5/16		Work continued as above. Continued fine weather.	
	3/5/16		do.	
	4/5/16		do.	
	5/5/16		do.	
	6/5/16		Lieut. T.C. Freeth transferred to 151st Field Co R.E. by order of C.R.E. 38th Division.	
	7/5/16		Work continued as on 1st May.	
	8/5/16		do.	
	9/5/16		do. 2nd Lieut C.S. Heaton-Armstrong joined from Base	
	10/5/16		do. Major J.W. Lanouly returned from leave of absence	
	11/5/16		do.	
	12/5/16		do.	
	13/5/16		do.	
	14/5/16		do.	
	15/5/16		do. No. 62849 Pion. A. Williams wounded by bullet.	

Army Form C. 2118

WAR DIARY
or
INTELLIGENCE SUMMARY
(Erase heading not required.)

Instructions regarding War Diaries and Intelligence Summaries are contained in F. S. Regs., Part II. and the Staff Manual respectively. Title Pages will be prepared in manuscript.

Place	Date	Hour	Summary of Events and Information	Remarks and references to Appendices
LAVENTIE	16/5/16		Work continued on MOATED GRANGE SECTION as follows Reclaiming Reserve Line Construction of Machine Gun Emplacements Wiring Boogerot Line, Construction of Support Line & Erection of dugouts.	
	17/5/16		do. Lieut J Howells & Sec Lieut J McLean proceeded to England on leave	
	18/5/16		do	
	19/5/16		do	
	20/5/16		do	
	21/5/16		do	
	22/5/16		do	
	23/5/16		do	
	24/5/16		do Sec Lieut A H Soutar proceeded to Scotland on leave.	
	25/5/16		do	
	26/5/16		do N° 874 SP Sapper J Barnett wounded in head. A bullet struck his steel helmet & glanced off inflicting a very slight wound. His life was probably saved by wearing the steel helmet.	
	27/5/16		do Lieut J Howells & Sec Lieut J McLean returned from leave.	

1875 Wt. W593/826 1,000,000 4/15 J.B.C. & A. A.D.S.S./Forms/C. 2118.

Army Form C. 2118

WAR DIARY
or
INTELLIGENCE SUMMARY
(Erase heading not required.)

Place	Date	Hour	Summary of Events and Information	Remarks and references to Appendices
LAVENTIE	28/5/16		Work continued as above.	
	29/5/16		do.	
	30/5/16		do. Following NCO + men wounded 62527 Lcd Corp. H C White 62569 Sapper H Jones 62602 " R Rose 62633 " SS Wood (at duty)	
	31/5/16		do. 1 Officer + 50 men of 1/3rd Field Co. RE(T) South Midland Division attached to the Company for work instruction	

J R Samonly
Major RE
OC 123rd Field Coy RE

Army Form C. 2118

WAR DIARY
or
INTELLIGENCE SUMMARY
(Erase heading not required.)

Instructions regarding War Diaries and Intelligence Summaries are contained in F. S. Regs., Part II. and the Staff Manual respectively. Title Pages will be prepared in manuscript.

Place	Date	Hour	Summary of Events and Information	Remarks and references to Appendices
LAVENTIE.	1st June 1916.		Work continued by Company on MOATED GRANGE SECTION. Following work in hand :— Reclamation of old Reserve line Construction of Concrete machine gun emplacements. Wiring Boesperot Line Construction of Support Line Erection of steel dugouts in Front line Extension of Great Eastern Tramway.	
	2/6/16		do.	
	3/6/16		do.	
	4/6/16.		do. See Lieut A.H. SOUTAR returned from leave.	
	5/6/16.		do.	
	6/6/16.		do.	
	7/6/16.		At night a new trench was dug across the reentrant south of Birdcage in "No mans land" Nos. 1 & 2 Sections engaged on the work with working parties of 300 infantry. The new trench was dug to an average depth of 18 inches Casualties No 67552 Lance Corpl # Jones wounded also 2 Killed and Five wounded from infantry working party	

WAR DIARY
or
INTELLIGENCE SUMMARY
(Erase heading not required.)

Army Form C. 2118

Place	Date	Hour	Summary of Events and Information	Remarks and references to Appendices
LAVENTIE	8/6/16		Work continued as on 1st June also deepening of new trench & wiring of same continued at night.	
	9/6/16		do.	
	10/6/16		do.	
	11/6/16		Instructions received that the Company will go back for rest and training with the 38th Division on the 12th inst and R.E. work on MOATED GRANGE SECTION to be handed over to 3/1 Field Co. RE(T) 61st (South Midland) Division.	
	12/6/16		Company moved from Laventie at 8 a.m. to L'ECLEME in 113th Brigade Group.	
	13/6/16		Company rested at L'ECLEME	
	14/6/16		Company moved to MAREST under orders of G.O.C. 113th Brigade.	
	15/6/16		Company moved to ABBAYE NEUVELLE FARME under orders of G.O.C. 113th Brigade.	

Army Form C. 2118

WAR DIARY
or
INTELLIGENCE SUMMARY

(Erase heading not required.)

Place	Date	Hour	Summary of Events and Information	Remarks and references to Appendices
ABBEYE NEUVELLE FERME	16/6/16		Company superintended digging of trenches on MONCHY BRETON Training Area. 2nd Lieut W.A. EVANS returned from hospital.	
	17/6/16		Training of Company in drill & demolition wiring etc commenced.	
	18/6/16		HOLIDAY	
	19/6/16		Training continued	
	20/6/16		do	
	21/6/16		do	
	22/6/16		do	
	23/6/16		do	
	24/6/16		Company took part in 113th Brigade Scheme.	
	25/6/16		Company took part in 38th Division Scheme.	
	26/6/16		Company moved at 5 pm under orders of G.O.C. 113th Bde. to MONCHEL & arrived at 12 midnight.	

Army Form C. 2118

WAR DIARY
or
INTELLIGENCE SUMMARY
(Erase heading not required.)

Instructions regarding War Diaries and Intelligence Summaries are contained in F. S. Regs., Part II. and the Staff Manual respectively. Title Pages will be prepared in manuscript.

Place	Date	Hour	Summary of Events and Information	Remarks and references to Appendices
MONCHEL	27/6/16		Company marched to RIBEAUCOURT at 6-45 pm under orders of G.O.C. 113th Bde.	
RIBEAUCOURT	28/6/16		Arrived in billets at RIBEAUCOURT at 3.45 am. at 1 pm orders received to leave billets at 4 pm for HERISSART. This was cancelled at 2-30 pm and orders received to stand fast for further instructions.	
	29/6/16		Company training	
	30/6/16		Orders received at 10 am to leave at 4 pm to billets at HERISSART. At 11 pm orders received that company will proceed to billets at PUCHEVILLERS instead.	

J.P Jamouly
Maj RE
O/C 123rd Fd Co RE

vol 8

Confidential

War Diary
of
123rd Field Coy R.E.
38th Welsh Div
July 1916

WAR DIARY
or
INTELLIGENCE SUMMARY
(Erase heading not required.)

Army Form C. 2118

Place	Date	Hour	Summary of Events and Information	Remarks and references to Appendices
PUCHEVILLERS	1st July 1916	12·45 am	Arrived at billets in PUCHEVILLERS at 12·45 am. MAJOR. I.W. LAMONBY became Acting C.R.E. as Colonel KNOX went to hospital. 3rd and 4th ARMIES attached German lines.	
		6·30 pm	LIEUT. J. HOWELLS took over command of company	
		6 pm	Received orders to be prepared to move tonight	
		11 pm	Received orders to move to TOUTENCOURT	
		12 pm	Marched to TOUTENCOURT.	
TOUTENCOURT	2nd		Arrived TOUTENCOURT.	
do.	3rd	5 pm	In billets at TOUTENCOURT. awaiting instructions.	
do.			Received instructions to move to MERICOURT L'ABBE at 5·30 pm.	
		8·30 pm	Marched to MERICOURT L'ABBE.	
MERICOURT L'ABBE	4th	12·30 am	Arrived MERICOURT L'ABBE	
do.	5th		In billets awaiting instructions. Heavy rain.	

Army Form C. 2118

WAR DIARY
or
INTELLIGENCE SUMMARY
(Erase heading not required.)

Instructions regarding War Diaries and Intelligence Summaries are contained in F. S. Regs., Part II. and the Staff Manual respectively. Title Pages will be prepared in manuscript.

Place	Date	Hour	Summary of Events and Information	Remarks and references to Appendices
MERICOURT L'ABBE.	5/7/16	1.40pm	Received instructions to proceed to relieve 95th FIELD Co. RE 27th DIVISION. at F.28.6.17 at 8-30 p.m.	
		6-30pm	Arrived at F.28.6.17 + relieved 95th Fd. Co. RE. Company billeted in dugouts.	
F.28.6.17.	6/7/16		Company in reserve. Remained in billets all day. LIEUT-COL. FALCON. RE. became C.R.E. MAJOR I.W.LAMONBY returned to take over command of company.	
"	7/7/16	2am	Received instructions to proceed to MINDEN POST and be there at 9 am. Company in reserve. 115TH BRIGADE attacked MAMETZ wood without success. HEAVY RAIN.	
"	8/7/16	1 am.	Received instructions to march company back to billets.	
"	"	2.30am	Arrived in billets.	
"	8/7/16	6-55pm	N°1 SECTION instructed to carry RE material to QUEEN'S NULLATT. in accordance with orders from C.R.E (CRE A.25. 8/7/16) N°3 SECTION instructed to repair bridges at CARNOY WOOD. (CRE A24 8/7/16	

WAR DIARY
or
INTELLIGENCE SUMMARY

(Erase heading not required.)

Army Form C. 2118

Instructions regarding War Diaries and Intelligence Summaries are contained in F. S. Regs., Part II. and the Staff Manual respectively. Title Pages will be prepared in manuscript.

Place	Date	Hour	Summary of Events and Information	Remarks and references to Appendices
F28, B, 1, 7.	9/7/16.		Company employed carrying material and forming dumps at QUEENS NULLAH and CATERPILLAR WOOD and in constructing foot road to POMMIERS REDOUBT.	
		10 pm	Received instructions from C.R.E. Company to take part in operations against MAMETZ WOOD on 10th inst. Company to be on West side of MAMETZ VILLAGE at 3 am.	
"	10/7/16	1.30 am	Company Paraded & marched to MAMETZ 139 NCO's & men. Strength 6 Officers and	
		2.40 am	Arrived MAMETZ VILLAGE.	
		3. am	O.C. reported to G.O.C. 113th Bde in DANTZIG ALLEY.	
		3.30 am	Artillery bombardment began.	
		4.15 am	16th Bn. R.W.F attacked MAMETZ WOOD	
		5.0 pm	Information received at 113th Bde H.Q. that our troops had reached the wood and were pushing on.	
		6.40 am	Received orders from G.O.C. 113th Bde to move 2 Sections forward to QUEENS NULLAH. Nos 1-4 Sections moved forward.	

WAR DIARY
or
INTELLIGENCE SUMMARY
(Erase heading not required.)

Army Form C. 2118

Place	Date	Hour	Summary of Events and Information	Remarks and references to Appendices
	10/7/16	7.3 am	O.C. ordered remainder of Company to be moved forward to QUEENS NULLAH.	
		7.5 am	Information received that the first objective had been reached. A line running short of the ride running east from WOOD SUPPORT.	
		7.10 am	O.C. 113th Bde asked me to win this line. I suggested that it would be much better to reconnoitre it first to which he agreed.	
		7.14 am	Moved forward to QUEENS NULLAH with O.C. 113th Bde and instructed Lieuts McLEAN and LETHBRIDGE to reconnoitre front line & if conditions were favourable to arrange with infantry for covering parties & to win the line at once.	
		7.45 am	Went forward to wood with C.S.M. of Company to see what work could be done. Went up trench on west side of wood to a point about 150 yards in the rear of the front line. Found infantry retiring having lost all their Officers. Reorganized them & took command until relieved at 9.30 am by MAJOR BELL 13th R.W.F.	

WAR DIARY
or
INTELLIGENCE SUMMARY
(Erase heading not required.)

Army Form C. 2118

Place	Date	Hour	Summary of Events and Information	Remarks and references to Appendices
	10/7/16	9.30am	Returned to south end of wood & found that Nos 1 & 4 SECTIONS had started wiring.	
		11-3.00am	Ordered Nos 2 & 3 Sections up to relieve Nos 1 & 4 as they had suffered several casualties.	
		2 pm	About 60 German Soldiers gave themselves up as prisoners & one man captured by the company could speak English and when I questioned him he informed me the enemy troops where were very few were completely demoralised, I therefore took him before the General Staff who again questioned him. It was then decided to attack.	
		3 pm	Wiring completed, & I was ordered to command all R.E.'s & Pioneers in the wood & hold them in reserve. There were 1½ Sections of 124th Field Co on the left flank, one company of 19th (Pioneer Bn) Welch Reg, & Section of 123rd Field Co R.E. in the centre & one company of 19th Pioneer Bn Welch Reg. on the right.	
		4.15pm	The attack started & was successful in reaching a line about 200 yards south of the northern edge of MAMETZ WOOD	

WAR DIARY
or
INTELLIGENCE SUMMARY
(Erase heading not required.)

Army Form C. 2118

Place	Date	Hour	Summary of Events and Information	Remarks and references to Appendices
	10/7/16	5:15 p.m.	Reconnaissance parties sent out to report on advisability of wiring front. It was decided by GOC 113th & 114th Bdes not to wire it as another advance was proposed at 8 p.m. Company therefore carried material to CROSS ROADS at points X.24.a.9.9¾.	
		5:30 p.m.	Ordered by G.O.C. to make strong point at X.24.a.7.9¾. So I sent up No.3 Section to do the job. Owing to heavy rifle & machine gun fire it was decided not to continue work on the point.	
		6 p.m.		
		8 p.m.	It was decided by G.O.C. not to attack tonight as the troops were very tired & few officers were left to take command.	
			Ordered by GOC 114th Bde to take company to south edge of wood and remain in reserve. Did so at once.	
		11 p.m.		
	11/7/16	2 a.m.	Proceeded with carrying party to HALTE & brought up rations for Company.	
		3 a.m.	Sent to Company H.Q. for all spare men to be sent up to the wood.	
		7 a.m.	Instructed by G.O.C. 115th Bde (who had taken over command)	

WAR DIARY
or
INTELLIGENCE SUMMARY
(Erase heading not required.)

Army Form C. 2118

Place	Date	Hour	Summary of Events and Information	Remarks and references to Appendices
		6 a.m.	to wire line V.W.X (on sketch map issued to troops) about No 3 Section to do this work. Lieutenants E.S.H. ARMSTRONG. with 32 trakemen corks etc arrived. Sent these men to assist No 3 Section in wiring. Started part of No 2 Section strengthening strong point at X.24.a.6.3.	
		8.30 a.m.	Inspected front line & considered it advisable to wire it. Reported to O.C. who instructed me to do it. Obtained 60 pioneers & put them on the work.	
		11.30 a.m.	No 3 Section completed wiring. (Pioneers completed wiring)	
		1 p.m.	Instructed Lieut LETHBRIDGE to take No 1 & 4 Sections back to billets.	
		2 p.m.	Instructed to hold Alexander & company in reserve at X.24.a.6.3. during a contemplated attack aimed for 3.30 p.m. This attack did not take place.	

WAR DIARY
or
INTELLIGENCE SUMMARY

(Erase heading not required.)

Army Form C. 2118

Place	Date	Hour	Summary of Events and Information	Remarks and references to Appendices
	17/7/16	6.30 p.m.	Lieut HOWELLS having arrived I handed over command to him & returned to billet.	
		9.30 p.m.	Lieut HOWELLS received instructions to proceed with all men to billets.	
		11 p.m.	All men back in billets. Following casualties sustained in the two days fighting.	
			Killed Lance Corp. D. Masters, Sapper A.J. Brooks, Sapper H. Bellis.	
			Died of wounds Sapper R.T. Williams	
			Wounded Lieutenant A.H. Soutar R.E., C.S.M. S. Evans, Sergeants R.P. Shefford, Sergeant J. Robson. Corporal W.J. Buck. Second Corp. S.T. Martyn. Lee Corp. W. Perry. Lee Corp. C.S. Walker. Lance Corp. C.P. Baldwyn.	
			Sappers J. Griffiths, D.J. Roach, E.G. Conor, J. Savery, C.R. Evans, J. Williams, C.H. Yonde, B. Hutchison, W. Birtles, R. Bell, A. Hood, S. Marshall, A.S. Clarke	

WAR DIARY or INTELLIGENCE SUMMARY

Army Form C. 2118

Place	Date	Hour	Summary of Events and Information	Remarks and references to Appendices
F28.B.17.	12/7/16.	10 a.m.	Received instructions from CRE 38th Div. to entrain supplies at MEAULTE at 7 p.m. for LONGPRE. Transport to proceed by road.	
		4 p.m.	Company left billets	
		6 p.m.	" arrived MEAULTE and found that no arrangements had been made for entraining	
		9 p.m.	Informed by staff officer that trains would arrive at 4 a.m. 13th to take company to LONGPRE.	
	13/7/16.	5 a.m.	Left for LONGPRE.	
		11 a.m.	Arrived LONGPRE. & informed we were to move to RUBEMPRE today.	
		8 p.m.	Left in buses for RUBEMPRE	
		10 p.m.	Arrived at " & found transport there

Army Form C. 2118

WAR DIARY
or
INTELLIGENCE SUMMARY
(Erase heading not required.)

Instructions regarding War Diaries and Intelligence Summaries are contained in F. S. Regs., Part II. and the Staff Manual respectively. Title Pages will be prepared in manuscript.

Place	Date	Hour	Summary of Events and Information	Remarks and references to Appendices
	14/7/16	9am	Received orders to move to ROSSIGNEL FARM.	
		1pm	Left RUBENPRE	
		6pm	Arrived ROSSIGNEL FARM. to relieve 1/1st South Midland Field Co.R.E.	
	15/7/16	—		
	16/7/16	9am	Took over work from 1/1st South Midland Field Co. Following jobs in hand (a) Rossignol Stores and workshops. (b) Repairing road from Coigneux to Courcelles	
	17/7/16		Reported on strong points in village of HEBURTERNE	
	18/7/16		300 infantry employed on roads (B)wires erected for 510 men at the DELL	
	19/7/16		Sites of proposed Trench Mortar Emplacements in front line Reconnoitred	
	20/7/16		100 men of RAMC. allotted to us for improvement of COIGNEUX — COURCELLES ROAD. Erected bivouacs for these men at the DELL.	

1875 Wt. W593/826 1,000,000 4/15 J.B.C. & A. A.D.S.S./Forms/C. 2118.

Army Form C. 2118

WAR DIARY
or
INTELLIGENCE SUMMARY
(Erase heading not required.)

Instructions regarding War Diaries and Intelligence Summaries are contained in F. S. Regs., Part II. and the Staff Manual respectively. Title Pages will be prepared in manuscript.

Place	Date	Hour	Summary of Events and Information	Remarks and references to Appendices
ROSSIGNEL FARM	21/7/16		Work started on Trench Mortar Emplacements in front line with 60. infantry. Nº 2 and 4 Sections moved to billets in COLINCAMPS	
	22/7/16		Reconnoitred YELLOW LINE with a view to improving it	
COLINCAMPS	23/7/16		Nº 1 SECTION and COMPANY H.R. moved to COLINCAMPS	
	24/7/16		Took over work from 69th & 70th Field Co's RE on area opposite COLINCAMPS. Right boundary Junction Q.4.20+21 Trenches. Left boundary Flag Avenue inclusive.	
	25/7/16		Handed over work on Trench Mortar Emplacements to 151st Field Co RE & continued work of 70th Field Co RE on 12' deep dugouts	
	26/7/16		Continued work on deep dugouts and started realigning front line & Communication Trenches	
	27/7/16		Work continued	
	28/7/16		do	
	29/7/16	12 noon	Handed over work on front line to 84th Field Co.	
		1 pm.	Marched to & bivouacked in BUS.	

Army Form C. 2118

WAR DIARY
or
INTELLIGENCE SUMMARY

(Erase heading not required.)

Instructions regarding War Diaries and Intelligence Summaries are contained in F.S. Regs., Part II. and the Staff Manual respectively. Title Pages will be prepared in manuscript.

Place	Date	Hour	Summary of Events and Information	Remarks and references to Appendices
	30/7/16	12 noon	Marched to and bivouacked in AUTHIEULE.	
	31/7/16	1-30am	Marched to DOULLENS NORTH STATION and entrained.	
		6-19am	Train left.	
		12-30pm	Arrived HOPOUTRE and detrained.	
		1-30pm	Marched to LEDRINGHEM.	
LEDRINGHEM.		10-30pm	Arrived & billeted in LEDRINGHEM.	

J. Hammond
Major R.E.

Original

Vol 9

War Diary August 1916.

123rd FIELD COMPANY
ROYAL ENGINEERS.

Confidential

Army Form C. 2118

WAR DIARY
or
INTELLIGENCE SUMMARY

128rd FIELD COMPANY
ROYAL ENGINEERS.

(Erase heading not required.)

Instructions regarding War Diaries and Intelligence Summaries are contained in F.S. Regs, Part II. and the Staff Manual respectively. Title Pages will be prepared in manuscript.

Place	Date	Hour	Summary of Events and Information	Remarks and references to Appendices
LEDRINGHEM.	1/8/16		Company resting in billets. Received orders from CRE 38th Division to report to Chief Engineer 2nd Army at Cassel on 2nd inst.	
	2/8/16		Reported to CE 2nd Army received instructions from him to build ammunition sheds at BAVINCHOVE, CAESTRE, STRAZEELE, and ABEELE, and to send one section to each place.	
	3/8/16		No 1 Section and Headquarters moved to BAVINCHOVE No 2 " " " CAESTRE No 3 " " " STRAZEELE No 4 " " " ABEELE.	
BAVINCHOVE			2/Lieut. LETHBRIDGE departed to CRE for instruction as ADJUTANT	
CAESTRE	4/8/16		Reported to CE 2nd Army. Company H.Q. moved to CAESTRE.	
	5/8/16		All sections at work. Received instructions from C.E. to stop work at BAVINCHOVE and move No 1 SECTION to CAESTRE. No 1 Section moved to Caestre at 7/-. reported to No 2 Section	
	6/8/16		20 men from RHA, 150 men RHA reported to No 1 Section, 100 men ASC reported to No 3 Section & No 4 Section	
	7/8/16		CRE 38th Division inspected work. 2/Lieut LETHBRIDGE returned to Company.	
	8/8/16		2/LIEUT ARMSTRONG transferred to 151st Field Co RE.	

1875 Wt. W593/826 1,000,000 4/15 J.B.C. & A. A.D.S.S./Forms/C. 2118.

Army Form C. 2118

WAR DIARY
or
INTELLIGENCE SUMMARY
(Erase heading not required.)

123rd FIELD COMPANY
ROYAL ENGINEERS.

Instructions regarding War Diaries and Intelligence Summaries are contained in F. S. Regs., Part II. and the Staff Manual respectively. Title Pages will be prepared in manuscript.

Place	Date	Hour	Summary of Events and Information	Remarks and references to Appendices
CAESTRE	9/8/16		Work continued on Ammunition sheds at CAESTRE, STRAZEELE and ABEELE.	
	10/8/16		do	
	11/8/16		do	
	12/8/16		do	
	13/8/16		No 1 SECTION moved to BOLLEZEELE No 2 SECTION ESQUELBECQ to build Baths for 38th Division their work at CAESTRE.	
	14/8/16		Work continued on ammunition sheds	
	15/8/16		do.	
	16/8/16		do.	
	17/8/16		do.	
	18/8/16		do.	
	19/8/16		do. LIEUT. HOWELLS proceeded to ESQUELBECQ to do special work for C.R.E.	
	20/8/16		do. Received instructions from C.E. 2nd Army that the company will rejoin the 38th Division + leave one officer + 9 N.C.Os + men behind to temp supervise work at ammunition sheds	

1875 Wt. W593/826 1,000,000 4/15 J.B.C. & A. A.D.S.S./Forms/C.2118.

Army Form C. 2118

123rd FIELD COMPANY
ROYAL ENGINEERS.

WAR DIARY
or
INTELLIGENCE SUMMARY
(Erase heading not required.)

Place	Date	Hour	Summary of Events and Information	Remarks and references to Appendices
CAESTRE	21/8/16		Received instructions to proceed to A.15.6.9.5. early on 22nd inst from CRE 38th Division. LIEUT HOWELLS returned to company. Received instructions from CE Dulbury to leave LIEUT SOUTAR + 9 men behind to finish work.	
CAESTRE	22/8/16		Received instructions to march N°s 2, 3 + 4 Sections to VLAMERTINGHE early in morning. N°1 Section to entrain + join them to bivouac on west side of the town until 9 p.m. then in evening to march to dugouts at C.25.d.0.7. on Canal Bank 1 mile north of YPRES. Transport to proceed to A.15.6.9.5. Left Caestre at 6.30 am + arrived at C.25.d.0.7 at 11pm.	
C.25.d.0.7. near YPRES	23/8/16		Transport moved to PESELHOEK. N°1 Section detailed to work for R.F.A. on Observation posts, Gun Emplacements and Trench Mortar Emplacements. Reconnoitred for Strong point at HILL TOP C.21.d.1.8. with CRE, GSOI, GSOII 38th DIVISION and II LIEUT W.A. EVANS in forenoon. In afternoon reconnoitred for Strong point at LA BELLE ALLIANCE C.21.C.1.7. with II LIEUT J.S. LETHBRIDGE. N°3 SECTION started work on HILL TOP Strong point with infantry working party of 30 men. N°4 SECTION started work on LA BELLE ALLIANCE Strong point with infantry working party of 60 men.	

Army Form C. 2118

WAR DIARY
or
INTELLIGENCE SUMMARY
(Erase heading not required.)

123rd FIELD COMPANY
ROYAL ENGINEERS.

Place	Date	Hour	Summary of Events and Information	Remarks and references to Appendices
CoSdO7 near YPRES	24/8/16		Reconnoitred WILSONS FARM C 26 & 51 for Strong points. Work started here by No 2 Section under SERGT. R.P. SHEPPARD with 30 infantry at night.	
	25/8/16		Work continued on Strong points at HILL TOP and LA BELLE ALLIANCE with Nos 3 & 4 Sections with working parties of 30 infantry from 115th Brigade.	
do.	26/8/16		Work continued on Strong points. Inspected WILSON FARM with MAJOR GENERAL BLACKADDER, CRE., & GSO1 38th DIVISION.	
do.			Work continued. Inspected HILL TOP & LA BELLE ALLIANCE with CRE 38th DIV.	
do.	27/8/16		Work continued as above.	
do.	28/8/16		do.	
do.	29/8/16		do. Heavy rain interfered with work.	
do.	30/8/16		do. Heavy rain interfered with work.	
do.	31/8/16		do.	

J. [signature]
Major R.E.
O/C 123rd FIELD COMPANY
ROYAL ENGINEERS.

Vol 10

War Diary
123rd Field Coy RE
September 1916

Army Form C. 2118

WAR DIARY
or
INTELLIGENCE SUMMARY
(Erase heading not required.)

Instructions regarding War Diaries and Intelligence Summaries are contained in F. S. Regs., Part II. and the Staff Manual respectively. Title Pages will be prepared in manuscript.

Place	Date	Hour	Summary of Events and Information	Remarks and references to Appendices
C25 d 07 near YPRES	1/9/16		Work continued on strong points at HILL TOP LA BELLE ALLIANCE and WILSON FARM. and screening YPRES — ELVERDINGHE Road.	
	2/9/16		do.	
	3/9/16		do.	
	4/9/16		do.	
	5/9/16		do.	
	6/9/16		do.	
	7/9/16		do.	
	8/9/16		do.	
	9/9/16		do.	
	10/9/16		do.	
	11/9/16		do.	
	12/9/16		do.	
	13/9/16		do. Handed over work on LA BELLE ALLIANCE to 151st FIELD Co RE and took over work on HILL TOP SECTOR	
	14/9/16		Work continued as above	
	15/9/16		do.	
	16/9/16		do.	
	17/9/16		do. Military Medals awarded to the following	

WAR DIARY
or
INTELLIGENCE SUMMARY

(Erase heading not required.)

Army Form C. 2118

Instructions regarding War Diaries and Intelligence Summaries are contained in F. S. Regs., Part II. and the Staff Manual respectively. Title Pages will be prepared in manuscript.

Place	Date	Hour	Summary of Events and Information	Remarks and references to Appendices
C75607. YPRES	18/9/16		NCO's for work at Maments Wood on 10th & 11th July 1916. 62644 SERGT. A.M. DARROCH 62537 SERGT R.A. CULVERWELL 62566 SERGT. W.P. LANGMAN. 67540 SERGT T.H. ROGERS. Work continued as above.	
	19/9/16		do. 2nd LIEUT W.A.EVANS proceeded on leave.	
	20/9/16		do.	
	21/9/16		do	
	22/9/16		do	
	23/9/16		do.	
	24/9/16		do.	
	25/9/16		do.	
	26/9/16		do	
	27/9/16		do. Handed over work on HILL TOP to 151st Fd C RE	
	28/9/16		do.	
	29/9/16		do. 2nd LIEUT LETHBRIDGE proceed on leave.	
	30/9/16		do 2nd Lieut Evans returned from leave and Major Lanmoby proceeded on leave.	O.C. 123 Fd Coy RE — J Howells Lt RE

1875 Wt. W593/826 1,000,000 4/15 J.B.C. & A. A.D.S.S./Forms/C. 2118.

"Vol II"

<u>Secret.</u>   <u>Confidential.</u>

<u>Original</u>
War Diary - October - 1916.
_____

123 Field Coy. R.E. (38th (Welsh) Divn.
_____

<u>31-10-1916.</u>

WAR DIARY or INTELLIGENCE SUMMARY

Army Form C. 2118

123rd FIELD COMPANY ROYAL ENGINEERS.

Place	Date	Hour	Summary of Events and Information	Remarks and references to Appendices
C25 d 07 YPRES	1/10/16		Work continued on reclamation of front line from B17 to Lancashire trench – Wilson Farm strong point. Artillery D.P.'s, gun emplacements, Trench mortars Emplacements Canal bank dugouts etc.	
	2/10/16		do. 2 Lt. W.A. EVANS sent to hospital	
	3/10/16		do.	
	4/10/16		do.	
	5/10/16		do.	
	6/10/16		do.	
	7/10/16		do.	
	8/10/16		do. 2 Lt. J.S. LETHBRIDGE returned from leave	
	9/10/16		do. 2 Officers and 107 NCO's & men attached to company from 114th Brigade. These men are to provide all RE working parties & no other parties are to be asked for.	
	10/10/16			
	11/10/16		do.	
	12/10/16		do. MAJOR I.W. LAMONBY returned from leave & took over command of the company	

Army Form C. 2118

123rd FIELD COMPANY
ROYAL ENGINEERS.

WAR DIARY
or
INTELLIGENCE SUMMARY
(Erase heading not required.)

Instructions regarding War Diaries and Intelligence Summaries are contained in F. S. Regs., Part II. and the Staff Manual respectively. Title Pages will be prepared in manuscript.

Place	Date	Hour	Summary of Events and Information	Remarks and references to Appendices
C25 d.0.7. YPRES	13/10/16			
	14/10/16		do.	
	15/10/16		do.	
	16/10/16		do.	
	17/10/16		do.	
	18/10/16		do. 2.Lt. W.A. EVANS returned to company from hospital.	
	19/10/16		do.	
	20/10/16		do.	
	21/10/16		do.	
	22/10/16		do.	
	23/10/16		do.	
	24/10/16		do.	
	25/10/16		do.	
	26/10/16		do.	
	27/10/16		do.	
	28/10/16		do.	
	29/10/16		do.	
	30/10/16		do. During the month the men suffered very much from sickness & a large number were admitted to hospital	
	31/10/16		do.	

Meynell, Major RE
O.C. 123rd Fd Co. R.E.

Secret Vol 12

Original
War Diary — November 1916

———

123rd Field Coy, Royal Engineers

38th (Welsh) Division

———

1.12.16.

Army Form C. 2118

WAR DIARY
or
INTELLIGENCE SUMMARY
(Erase heading not required.)

Place	Date	Hour	Summary of Events and Information	Remarks and references to Appendices
C25 d.o.7. YPRES	1/11/16		3 Sections of Company employed on the reclamation of York & Lancashire Trench; Atlas Trench — Construction of Wilson Farm Strong point Artillery O.Po.) Trench Mortar Emplacements, tramway and dugouts on the Canal bank. 1 Section at Peselhoek employed on horse standings.	
	2/11/16		Lieut J HOWELLS proceeded on leave	
	3/11/16		do	
	4/11/16		No 82423 Sapper L Morgan wounded by shrapnel. Nine Reinforcements arrived from base.	
	5/11/16		do	
	6/11/16		do	
	7/11/16		do	
	8/11/16		do	
	9/11/16		do	
	10/11/16		do	
	11/11/16		do	
	12/11/16		Lieut J HOWELLS returned from leave	
	13/11/16		Received instructions from CRE to attach 2 NCOs	
	14/11/16		+ 10 Sappers to 14th Bn Welch Regiment to train for a raid on	

WAR DIARY
or
INTELLIGENCE SUMMARY

Army Form C. 2118

Place	Date	Hour	Summary of Events and Information	Remarks and references to Appendices
			HIGH COMMAND REDOUBT. Following men selected 62501 SERGT. R.P. SHEPPARD, 82587 CORP. W.R. FERRIS. Sappers. 67511 W.T. DOWN, 106105 M.J DAVIES, 82422 E. MORGAN 82423 L. MORGAN, 82452 J. BARNETT, 62595 Ed. WILLIAMS 82419 R. MARTIN, 92519 D.J ROACH, 82481 C. OBORNE 67556 L. PICKERING,	
	15/11/16		Raiding party trained in the fact they has to undertake in raid.	
	16/11/16		do do tested all demolition Material for raid.	
	17/11/16		do do 17th Bn Welch Reg attacked High Command Redoubt along with party of Sappers at 11pm, overrunned in enemy trenches for half an hour. Sappers captured a Sergeant Major & 6 men also a machine gun and periscope and a quantity of papers, reports & maps.	

WAR DIARY
or
INTELLIGENCE SUMMARY

(Erase heading not required.)

Army Form C. 2118

Place	Date	Hour	Summary of Events and Information	Remarks and references to Appendices
	18/11/16		Sappers demolished 2 enemy observation posts, one concrete machine gun and breached the parapet with guncotton. On returning Sapper J BARNETT was wounded in the face.	
	19/11/16.		Work carried on as on 18th inst.	
	20/11/16		do. 2nd LIEUT (TEMP. CAPT.) A. RUSSELL joined the Company. LIEUT. G McLEAN proceeded on leave.	
	21/11/16.		do.	
	22/11/16.		do.	
	23/11/16		do.	
	24/11/16		do	
	25/11/16.		do. 62501 Sergt R.P. SHEPPARD and 82567	

WAR DIARY
or
INTELLIGENCE SUMMARY

(Erase heading not required.)

Army Form C. 2118

Place	Date	Hour	Summary of Events and Information	Remarks and references to Appendices
	26/11/16		CORP. W.R. FERRIS. awarded the MILITARY MEDAL for gallantry on the 17th — met on the attack on High Command Redoubt.	
	27/11/16		do.	
	28/11/16		do.	
	29/11/16		do.	
	30/11/16		do. LIEUT. G McLEAN returned from leave.	

J. Kennedy
Maj. R.G.

S E C R E T

123 Field Coy
R.E.
Nov 1916.

H.Q.
114th Brigade
───────────

   Three N.C.O's and nine Sappers of the 123rd Field Company, R.E. took part in the raid on HIGH COMMAND REDOUBT last night, the 17th instant. They were all employed on demolition work. I have questioned each N.C.O. and man, and from the information they have given me I beg to report as follows :-

   The Sappers entered in 2 parties. The Right party of 2 N.C.O's and 5 Sappers under the command of SERGEANT R.P.SHEPPARD followed immediately behind Z (Right) Party of the Raiders. The Left Party of 1 N.C.O. and 4 Sappers under CORPORAL W.R.FERRIS followed behind X (Left) Party. SERGEANT SHEPPARD'S Party came across a Machine Gun Emplacement in what was generally supposed to be the Support Line: it had recently been built, and the centreing was still in position. A charge of 16 lbs of Guncotton was placed in the loophole and tamped. A Sketch of this M.G.E. is attached marked 'A'.

   About 10 yards away they found an O.P. - Sketch attached marked 'B'. SERGEANT SHEPPARD entered this O.P. following by his men. They found seven Germans, one being a Sergt. Major. These men were taken prisoners, and were handed over to an Infantry Party, who took them back to our lines. Two charges each of 16 lbs of Guncotton were placed here. There were 8 armoured cables leading into the Dugout. The Sappers found a quantity of papers and maps, also a periscope, which was unscrewed from the wall. These articles were handed over to the Infantry.

   CORPORAL FERRIS' Party proceeded to the Left with instructions to make a breach in the parapet, and also to demolish anything else of importance. One charge of 32 lbs. of Guncotton was placed in a hole in the highest part of the parapet. Section attached marked 'C'. An Observation Cupola was found a short distance away, and a charge placed against it. Sketch of Cupola is attached marked 'D'.

   A concrete Dugout about 8 ft. square inside, 4 yards away had been demolished by a Shell. After placing the charges CORPORAL FERRIS and his men made a search in the immediate vicinity and found a Machine Gun in an open emplacement on the parapet. They took it out, and as they had instructions to hand everything over to the Infantry they called the nearest man and told him to take it back. At this time a German rose up from the ground, where he had been lying, and advanced on CORPORAL FERRIS, who knocked him out with his knobkerry.

   Instructions had been given that the fuses had to be lit on the sounding of the third whistle, when all the Infantry men would be clear of the German trenches. All charges were successfully exploded, and considering the

sizes

sizes of the works and the quantity of the explosive used I feel certain that the demolitions were successful.

All the R.E. returned safely to our Lines, but one man, SAPPER J.BARNETT, was wounded by a Shell on the Trench Grids between D.20 and TURCO FARM.

                                                        (sd) J.W.LAMONBY,
                                                            Major R.E.,
18/11/1916.   O.C. 123rd Field Coy. R.E.

A.
Reinforced concrete Machine Gun Emplacement.

(Diagram: plan view of emplacement with 6'-0" interior width, 2'-6" wall thickness, 6'-0" depth, door on lower left, charge placed at upper wall)

- Charge

2'-6"
6'-0"
6'-0"
Door

Height inside 4'-0"
Roof 3'-0" thick.

38th (Welsh) Division
20-11-16.

B.

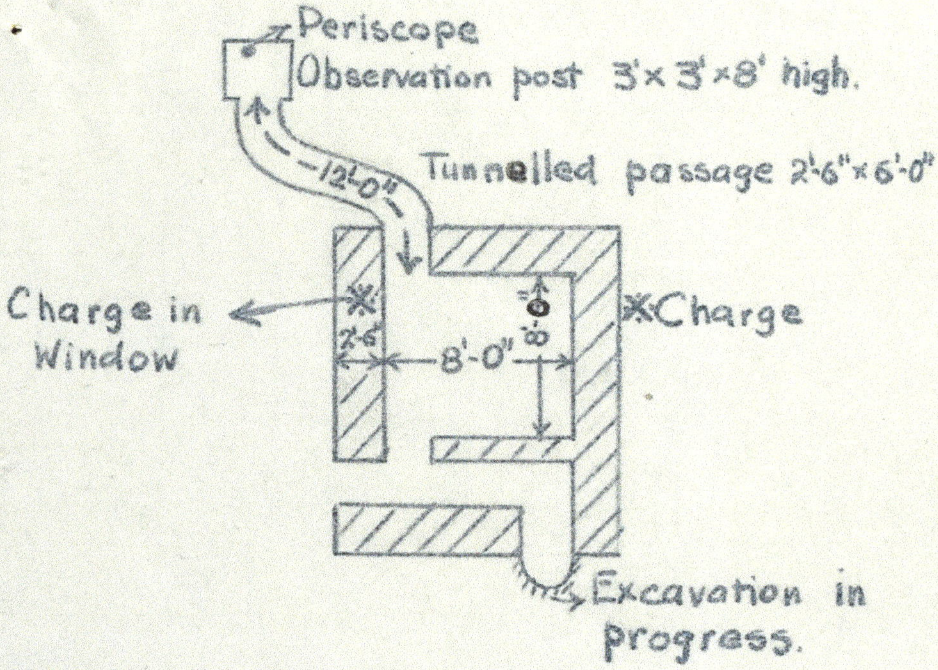
Periscope
Observation post 3'×3'×8' high.
12'-0"
Tunnelled passage 2'-6"×6'-0"
Charge in Window
2'-6"
8'-0"
8'-0"
※Charge
Excavation in progress.

Reinforced Concrete Dugout & O.P.

Height inside 5'-0"

Roof total thickness 4'-0"

Position of charges shown thus ※

38th (Welsh) Division
20-11-16.

C.

Section of German Parapet.

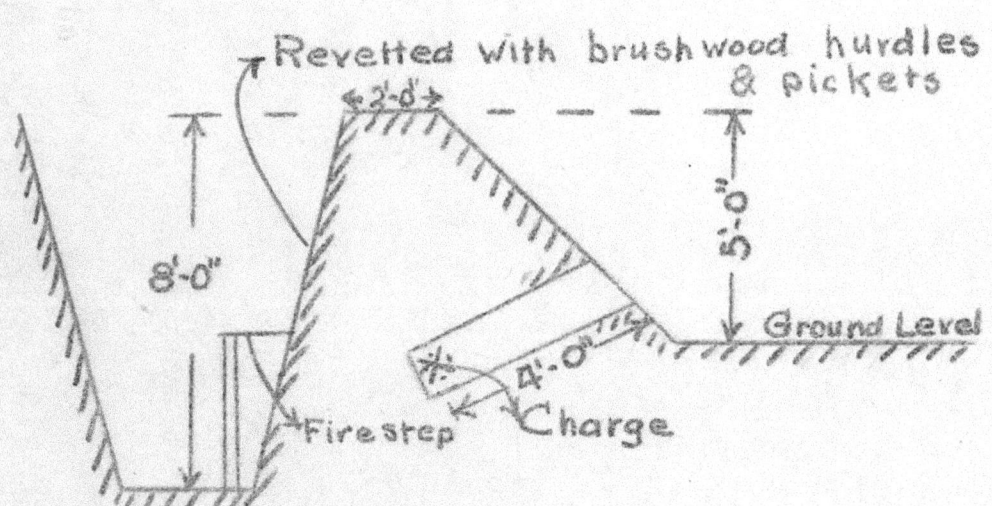

38th (Welsh) Division.
20-11-16

D.
Concrete O.P.

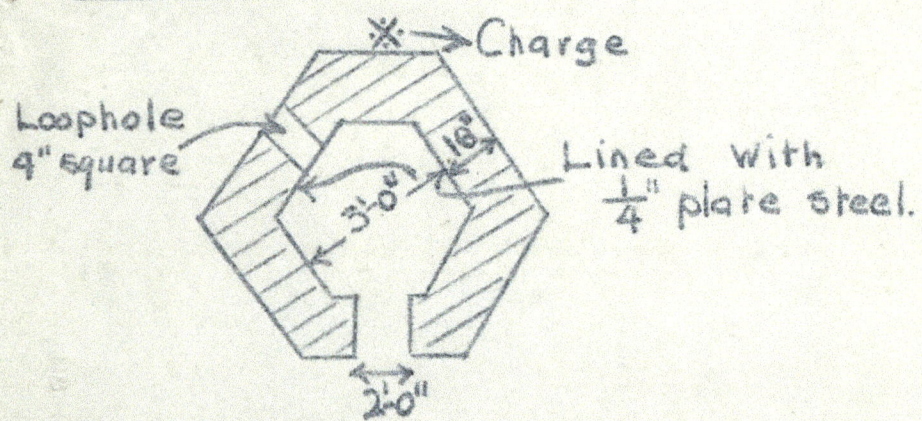

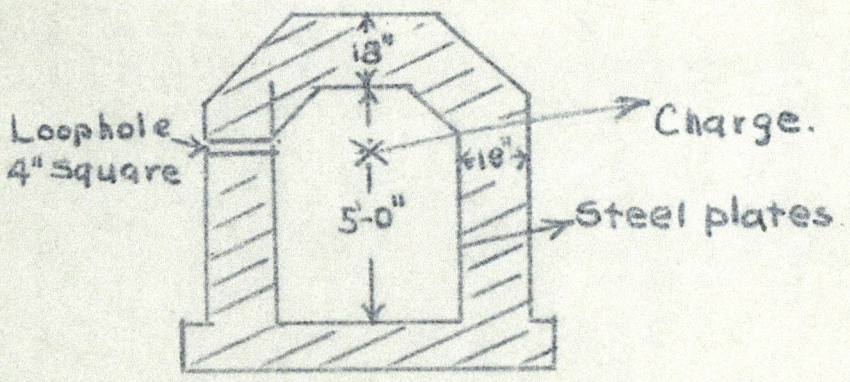

38th (Welsh) Division.
20-11-16.

SECRET.

Vol /3

Original

War Diary – December 1916

123rd Field Co. Royal Engineers

38th (Welsh) Division

31.12.1916

123rd FIELD COMPANY ROYAL ENGINEERS.

Army Form C. 2118

WAR DIARY or INTELLIGENCE SUMMARY

Place	Date	Hour	Summary of Events and Information	Remarks and references to Appendices
YPRES C25a07	1/12/16		Three sections of Company reclaiming York Lane Trench. Constructing Wilson Farm Strong points, Artillery O.P's. Trench Mortar Emplacements, Tramway, dugouts on Canal Bank. One section at horse lines at PESELHOEK.	
	2/12/16		do LT. J. HOWELLS transferred to 213th A.T. Coy R.E.	
	3/12/16		do	
	4/12/16		do	
	5/12/16		do	
	6/12/16		do	
	7/12/16		do	
	8/12/16		do	
	9/12/16		do	
	10/12/16		do	
	11/12/16		Received orders to relieve 234th Field Co R.E. in BOESINGHE SECTOR - All Company moved to billets at A 18 C.2.8.	

… FIELD COMPANY
ROYAL ENGINEERS.

Army Form C. 2118

WAR DIARY
or
INTELLIGENCE SUMMARY
(Erase heading not required.)

Instructions regarding War Diaries and Intelligence Summaries are contained in F. S. Regs., Part II. and the Staff Manual respectively. Title Pages will be prepared in manuscript.

Place	Date	Hour	Summary of Events and Information	Remarks and references to Appendices
A16 b.28.	12/12/16		Company meeting	
	13/12/16		All company employed on works in front line and on communications. Our front line is on the west bank of the YSER CANAL and the enemy's on the east side opposite the village of BOESINGHE. The Belgian Army is on our immediate left.	
	14/12/16		do.	
	15/12/16		do.	
	16/12/16			
	17/12/16			
	18/12/16			
	19/12/16			
	20/12/16			
	21/12/16			
	22/12/16			
	23/12/16			
	24/12/16			
	25/12/16		Christmas Day. Company had holiday	

WAR DIARY or INTELLIGENCE SUMMARY

123rd FIELD COMPANY ROYAL ENGINEERS.

Army Form C. 2118

Place	Date	Hour	Summary of Events and Information	Remarks and references to Appendices
ABC 26	26/10/16		do	
	27/10/16		do	
	28/10/16		do	
	29/10/16		Received orders to move to rest to WATTEN on 30th inst. 124th Field Co to relieve us. Men to proceed by rail from POPERINGHE at 10-30pm. Transport to move by road. Billet for the night at HERZEELE HOUTKERQUE.	
	30/10/16		Company moved as ordered. Cyclists left by road at 9 a.m.	
	31/10/16		Dismounted men arrived WATTEN at 4-20 am. Transport arrived 3 pm	

J Mumgly RE
O/C 123rd FIELD COMPANY
ROYAL ENGINEERS.

Vol 14

SECRET

Original
War Diary – January 1917.

123rd. Field Co, Royal Engrs.
38th (Welsh) Division

31.1.1916.

Army Form C. 2118

WAR DIARY
or
INTELLIGENCE SUMMARY

128rd FIELD COMPANY ROYAL ENGINEERS.

Place	Date	Hour	Summary of Events and Information	Remarks and references to Appendices
WATTEN, FRANCE	1/1/17		During rest period the following training was carried out :- Squad drill with and without arms, Rifle exercises, Musketry, Extended order and Bayonet fighting, Physical training, Company Drill. Military Engineering. Knotting, Lashing, Setting out work, Extending working parties, Use of "W" tube, Field level, Pontoons and Weldon Trestle. G.S. Mounted Section were also trained in Section Drill.	
	2/1/17		Training as above. Lieut. A.K. Locker returned from leave.	
	3/1/17		do — Major I.W. Lamonly to England for Senior Officers Course at ALDERSHOT.	
	4/1/17		do — Captain A. RUSSELL assumed command.	
	5/1/17		do — Lieut. W.A. EVANS proceeded on leave.	
	6/1/17		do —	
	7/1/17.		Sunday. Company resting after 9 am. Parade. 2nd Lieut. W. DICKINSON joined Company from BASE.	

WAR DIARY
or
INTELLIGENCE SUMMARY
(Erase heading not required.)

Army Form C. 2118
123rd FIELD COMPANY
ROYAL ENGINEERS.

Place	Date	Hour	Summary of Events and Information	Remarks and references to Appendices
WATTEN.	8/11/17		Training in subject mentioned at on 1st instant.	
FRANCE	9/11/17		do	
	10/11/17		do	
	11/11/17		do — Received orders to move to CANAL BANK at C.26.d.0.7 (one mile N. of YPRES) to relieve 234th Field Coy R.E. Men to proceed by rail. Transport by road, halting for night at HOUTKERQUE.	
C.25.d.0.7. YPRES.	12/11/17		Company proceeded by rail from WATTEN at 10.a.m. arriving CANAL BANK 6-30 p.m. No 3 Section detailed for work at L2 (B.23.c.6.4.) under VIII th Corps, returning to PEZELHOEK for billets. Remaining sections detailed as under:— No 1. Section. (Reclaiming Y & b Trench & CHEER Trench (FRONT LINE) & construction of Concrete Company H.Q'rs. No 2. Section. Maintenance of Tramway from Dump (B.30.b.2.2.) to front line (C.21.d.9.6.) Additional accommodation & repair to existing dugouts in CANAL BANK. No 4. Section. Continuation of strongpoint at WILSON FARM (C.26.e.5.0.) & Heavy Trench Mortar at FARGATE. Work for artillery commenced. — O.P.s Gun P.ts. etc.	

Army Form C. 2118

129rd FIELD COMPANY
ROYAL ENGINEERS.

WAR DIARY
or
INTELLIGENCE SUMMARY
(Erase heading not required.)

Instructions regarding War Diaries and Intelligence Summaries are contained in F.S. Regs., Part II. and the Staff Manual respectively. Title Pages will be prepared in manuscript.

Place	Date	Hour	Summary of Events and Information	Remarks and references to Appendices
C.20.d.07.	13/1/17		Work carried on as mentioned on 12th inst.	
YPRES	14/1/17		do	
	15/1/17		do	
	16/1/17		do — Major M.S. HANMER. 3/1st WELSH Field Coy R.E. attached for instruction from ENGLAND.	
	17/1/17		do —	
	18/1/17		do —	
	19/1/17		do — Lieut. W.A. EVANS returned from leave.	
	20/1/17		do —	
	21/1/17		do —	
	22/1/17		do — Lieut. J. Lethbridge proceeded on leave.	
	23/1/17		do —	
	24/1/17		do —	
	25/1/17		do —	
	26/1/17		do — No 1 Section proceed to PESELHOEK to relieve No 3 Section on same work at L.2. No 3 Section joined at CANAL BANK to take over work on additional accommodation from No 2 Section. No 2 Section took over work on FRONT LINE.	
	27/1/17		Work carried on.	

Army Form C. 2118

WAR DIARY
or
INTELLIGENCE SUMMARY
(Erase heading not required.)

128rd FIELD COMPANY ROYAL ENGINEERS.

Instructions regarding War Diaries and Intelligence Summaries are contained in F. S. Regs., Part II. and the Staff Manual respectively. Title Pages will be prepared in manuscript.

Place	Date	Hour	Summary of Events and Information	Remarks and references to Appendices
C.25.d.07.	28/1/17		Work carried on mentioned on 27 th instant.	
YPRES.	29/1/17		do — Major M.S. HANMER returned to England.	
	30/1/17		do — Heavy shelling of CANAL BANK.	
	31/1/17		do —	

1875 Wt. W593/826 1,000,000 4/15 T.D.C. & A. A.D.S.S./Forms/C. 2118.

Secret Vol 15

Original
War Diary – February 1917.

123rd Field Co. Royal Engineers
38th (Welsh) Division.

28:2:1917.

123rd FIELD COMPANY ROYAL ENGINEERS.

WAR DIARY or INTELLIGENCE SUMMARY

Army Form C. 2118

Place	Date	Hour	Summary of Events and Information	Remarks and references to Appendices
C.25.d.07. YPRES.	1/2/17		Three sections of company employed reclaiming YORK & LANCS Trench, Strong point at WILSON FARM, Trench Works Emplace Artillery O.P.S, Battalion H.Q's LABRIQUE, Company H.Q? CLIFFORD TOWERS and Dugouts at CROSS ROADS FARM. Tramways & Dugouts on Canal Bank. One section at PESELHOEK working on L2 Defences B.23.a.9.5. (NOVARA FARM). F. Lieut. J. S. Kethbridge returned from leave	
	2/2/17		do —	
	3/2/17		do —	
	4/2/17		do —	
	5/2/17		do —	
	6/2/17		do —	
	7/2/17		do —	
	8/2/17		do —	
	9/2/17		do —	

123rd FIELD COMPANY ROYAL ENGINEERS.

Army Form C. 2118

WAR DIARY
or
INTELLIGENCE SUMMARY
(Erase heading not required.)

Instructions regarding War Diaries and Intelligence Summaries are contained in F. S. Regs., Part II. and the Staff Manual respectively. Title Pages will be prepared in manuscript.

Place	Date	Hour	Summary of Events and Information	Remarks and references to Appendices
C.25.d.0.7.	10/4/17		Work as for 1st instant.	
YPRES.	11/4/17		do	
	12/4/17		do — Major J.C.I. WOOD R.E. took over command of Company.	
	13/4/17		do — Major J.C.I. Wood proceeded on a course of instruction.	
	14/4/17		do	
	15/4/17		do	
	16/4/17		do	
	17/4/17		do	
	18/4/17		do — 2nd Lieut. W. Dickinson to G.O. School for course.	
	19/4/17		do	
	20/4/17		do — Work taken over from 227th Field Coy	
	21/4/17		R.E. in consequence of their rejoining 39th Division:—	
			A. TURCO FARM (Strong Point)	
			B. Electrical installation at HILL TOP (Strong Point).	
			Work in consequence ceased at WILSON FARM, CROSS ROADS and LA BRIQUE.	

WAR DIARY or INTELLIGENCE SUMMARY

123rd FIELD COMPANY ROYAL ENGINEERS.

Army Form C. 2118

Place	Date	Hour	Summary of Events and Information	Remarks and references to Appendices
C.26.d.07. YPRES.	23/2/17.		Work as previously described. 2/Lt Dickinson returned from Gas Course. Corpl. Walker kept "Home" to Divisional School for course of instruction.	
Hill Top Sector	23/2/17 24/2/17 25/2/17 26/2/17 27/2/17		do do do do do Major J.S. Wood O.C. returned from leave. O.C. visited I+L Trench O.C. visited Hill Top. Brigade change. Divisional boundary changed right now runs from Forward Cottage including Hill Top but excluding IRISH Farm and WILSON Farm to Bridge 2A. — do —	
	28/2/17		O.C. visited "Z1Z1" (enfilade battery) and O.P. No7 EUSE Farm. C.R.E visited sector. do	

J. Wood Major R.E.
O.C. 123 Field Co. R.E.

SECRET

Vol 16

Original

War Diary – March 1917.

123rd Field Co, Royal Engineers

38th (Welsh) Division

31-3-1917

WAR DIARY
or
INTELLIGENCE SUMMARY   123 Field Coy R.E.

Army Form C. 2118

Place	Date	Hour	Summary of Events and Information	Remarks and references to Appendices
C 25 d 0.7. Canal Bank N. of YPRES	1.3.17		No 3 Section rechaining YORK + LANCS Trench, constructing coy. H.Q. at CLIFFORD TOWERS and WILLOWS. No 4 Section TURCO Farm Strong Point, T.M. emplacement VIEW Fm. Work on R.A. at "2121" + JOYEUSE Fm. O.P. No 1 Section Tramways + dugouts on Canal Bank. No 2 Section at PESELHOEK working on L2 Defences. NOVARA Fm. Electric light maintained at HILLTOP also power pump installed.	B 23.9.5.
"	2nd	5am onwards	ST DAVIDS DAY. Brigade conference 11.30 a.m. re anti gas orders O.C. visit TURCO; + site for new T.M. at VIEW Fm + site for heavy artillery Intelligence 3 pm	
"	3rd		work as on 1st — do —	
"	4th	slight frost at night	— do — all horseshoeing tested all sections carried up to park animals for section + attached infantry for experiment. Dump at Railway Cottage shelled 5 to 7 pm	
"	5th	5 a.m. than frosty	cpl PARAMOUNTAIN wounded at dump. O.C. visit Y+L + TURCO. Dump again shelled 7.30 am. Lt Mc Lean to C.R.E. Yard PESELHOEK CR.E. at Canal Bank.	
"	6th		D.D.M.S. site chosen for Aid post at WILLOWS for duty	

WAR DIARY
INTELLIGENCE SUMMARY

Army Form C. 2118
123rd FIELD COMPANY ROYAL ENGINEERS

Place	Date	Hour	Summary of Events and Information	Remarks and references to Appendices
C 25 d 07 YPRES	7-3-17		Work as on 1st. O.C. visited HILLTOP testing petrol pump. Safety to line at HILLTOP ready to start up electric light plant if required. Extending wood line for mining truck to BUFFS & BOUNDARY Rds. report on PILKEM Rd. tramline to C.R.E. Work as on 1st. Capt RUSSELL inspecting camps re fire precautions.	
"	8		"S"	
"	9		O.C. Mr LETHBRIDGE left by train for ENGLAND on transfer to INDIA C.R.E. at Canal Bank	
"	10		Brigade change 114 take over right sector	
"	11	9 am 10 am 2pm	T. McM replacement view form fixing angle of bed on site. Trial of petrol pump at Hilltop (pump refused to start) Conference with Brigadier fixing site for Nissen hut	
"	12	9.30 am 11 pm	Inspection of bridges on Canal & exits from saps on wide site of Canal Bank inspecting TURCO with CO 14th & 15th WELSH in defence of TURCO strong point	

WAR DIARY
or
INTELLIGENCE SUMMARY

(Erase heading not required.)

Army Form C. 2118

123rd FIELD COMPANY
ROYAL ENGINEERS.

Instructions regarding War Diaries and Intelligence Summaries are contained in F. S. Regs., Part II. and the Staff Manual respectively. Title Pages will be prepared in manuscript.

Place	Date	Hour	Summary of Events and Information	Remarks and references to Appendices
C25 d.0.7 YPRES	13/3/1917		Work as on 1st	
"	14/3/1917		"	
	15	6pm	" except sections change round 2 sqnrs & 3 (Bn change) OC & Capt RUSSELL to Bgde Gillets - inspect horselines etc Battery men dump; shelled with 5.9's - FOCH FARM worked 15 marking out line of new infront of gfs line	
	16		IRISH FARM	
	17		" " Infantry work on PONDCOT. SALIENT m.G. emps. on coyal hqrtr British 1 airoplane brought down near BURNT FARM occupants landed safely	
	18		work as on 15th	

WAR DIARY or INTELLIGENCE SUMMARY

Army Form C. 2118

123rd FIELD COMPANY ROYAL ENGINEERS.

Place	Date	Hour	Summary of Events and Information	Remarks and references to Appendices
C25d.0.7 YPRES	19		Work as on 15th. Capt RUSSELL inspecting damaged 4" main	A 28
"	20		2nd Lt. LLOYD W.H. joined for duty at back billets (no question)	
"	21	4.30am	OC inspects wire in front of X line. Capt RUSSELL inspects damaged main at 30 C122 battery near Railway Cottage dump again shelled all day, railway C.R.E. visits Canal bank defences at POND COTTAGE & insufficient cover.	
"	22	4.15am	raid on 124 full to action	
		8.0am	Total hoped mud scoop on horse cannot lift earth from natural	
		11.0am	surface, but can move dry earth. handle too cov.	
"	23	pm.	work as on 15th O.C. to horse lines & stables at BRIELEN	
"	24		work as on 15th	

WAR DIARY
or
INTELLIGENCE SUMMARY

(Erase heading not required.)

Army Form C. 2118

123rd FIELD COMPANY
ROYAL ENGINEERS.

Instructions regarding War Diaries and Intelligence Summaries are contained in F.S. Regs., Part II. and the Staff Manual respectively. Title Pages will be prepared in manuscript.

Place	Date	Hour	Summary of Events and Information	Remarks and references to Appendices
C 25.d.0.7 YPRES	25/3/17		Works on 15th. attached infantry 22 & 23 from each Bn instead of 20 from. Lt WILLIAMS 10th WELSH still in charge. 2 electric alarm bells fitted at HILL TOP Pm. Infant work on Canal bank with C.R.E. Lt EVANS to GAS SCHOOL for gas course.	
"	26		Works as on 15th	rainy morning
"	27		Tested all arrangements for demolitions of bridges in Loyauen "working parties in back area during night (postponed)	
"	28		Work as on 15th except no working parties in frontline from 12 M.N. to 4 am. Torpedo failed to fire C.R.E. testing leads & detonators. leads faulty, after being dragged thro' wire	rain
"	29		2 CH. S.C. MORRIS & Sapper M.H.E. LITTLER firing Bangalore torpedo to fire	fine
"	30		Raid of trench TURCO 1 prisoner taken, raid successful, pertinent, no casualties.	
"	31		Inspection of sector by C in C Commander	J Wood Major O/C 123 Fd Coy

1875. Wt. W593/826 1,000,000 4/15 J.B.C. & A. A.D.S.S./Forms/C. 2118.

Secret.

Original
War Diary – April 1917.

123 Field Co. Royal Engrs.
38 (Welsh) Division.

30-4-17.

WAR DIARY or INTELLIGENCE SUMMARY

Army Form C. 2118

123rd FIELD COMPANY ROYAL ENGINEERS

Place	Date	Hour	Summary of Events and Information	Remarks and references to Appendices
YPRES HILLTOP SECTOR	1-4-17	10am	Conference with Brigadier Gen. 113 Bn. re working parties. No 1 Section under Lt DICKINSON reclaiming frontline Y+h trench north of TURCO constructing Coy HQ. at WILLOWS + Aid Post windows. No 2 Section Lt SOUTAR TURCO FARM Strong Point deep dugout and driving fire trench from No 2 to No 3 M.G. Electric lighting at HILLTOP. No 3 Section Lt EVANS CANAL BANK + Tramway maintenance. Constructing Divl. Baths superintending Canal bank defences + POND FARM Salient. No 4 Section Lt LLOYD L2 Defences under VIIIth Corps.	C 25 d 07
"	2-4-17		work as 1st	
"	3-4-17	7pm	Snowing heavily. OC visited X line mine with Brigadier Gen 113. Work as on 1st	
"	4-4-17		work stopped on Y+h trench owing to expected operation.	
"		15pm	OC visited post H1 + heading of Y+h with Capt RUSSELL + Section officer. also TURCO	

Army Form C. 2118

WAR DIARY
or
INTELLIGENCE SUMMARY
(Erase heading not required.)

123rd FIELD COMPANY
ROYAL ENGINEERS.

Instructions regarding War Diaries and Intelligence Summaries are contained in F. S. Regs., Part II. and the Staff Manual respectively. Title Pages will be prepared in manuscript.

Place	Date	Hour	Summary of Events and Information	Remarks and references to Appendices
YPRES HILLTOP SECTOR	5.4.17		Work as on 1st	
		9pm	CRE visited Canal bank fixing line of second wire in front of X line	
"	6.		Work as on 1st	
		10am	GOC 38 Div inspects M.G. Emp. on west canal bank also Brigade Battle H.Q.	fine
"	7.		Work as on 1st	
		10am	Test gas alarm	fine
			OC + Capt RUSSELL visit home lines	
"	8.		Work as on 1st	
"	9.		"	
"	10.		Brigade change CRE at Canal bank No 1 section to go to work at PESELHOEK	
"	11.		" 114 take over	
			" march to "	
			OC + Capt Russell to CARDOEN FARM 151 Fd Co re footbridge & track villets accommodation for No 1 Section p.m. rain turning to sleet + snow!	

WAR DIARY
or
INTELLIGENCE SUMMARY
(Erase heading not required.)

Army Form C. 2118

128rd FIELD COMPANY
ROYAL ENGINEERS.

Instructions regarding War Diaries and Intelligence Summaries are contained in F.S. Regs., Part II. and the Staff Manual respectively. Title Pages will be prepared in manuscript.

Place	Date	Hour	Summary of Events and Information	Remarks and references to Appendices
YPRES	12/4/17		Work as on 1st except on Y & L Trench. Lt DICKINSON + No 1 Section to Back billets for work in C.Rys. Yard PESELHOEK	cold strong wind
HILLTOP SECTOR	13		Work as on 12th. Visit from Staff Capt R.E. went round work at TURCO WILLOWS HILLTOP & frontline trenches.	
	14		Work as on 12th	
	15		" OC visited Zi Zi with Lt McLEAN & inspected gun pits at Parking batteries. Tested engine & pump HILL TOP	
	16		" visit from office of 227 field coy R.E. fixing of appointment with OC 227.	
	17		Handed over to 227 Field Coy R.E. Billets + all work south of Bridge & inclusive except Bathurst Canal Bank + Ext + pump at HILLTOP Coy moved to dugouts on E side of canal at 3 b bridge	

WAR DIARY or INTELLIGENCE SUMMARY

Army Form C. 2118

128rd FIELD COMPANY ROYAL ENGINEERS.

Place	Date	Hour	Summary of Events and Information	Remarks and references to Appendices
YPRES CANAL BANK E Side near Bridge 3/6	18/4/17		Nos 1 & 4 Sections as before. No 2 section HILLTOP Electric lighting & pumping set & making dugouts, shell proof on Canal Bank. No 3 section taking over Tramway at AUSTERLITZ dump + supervision of work on Coy HQs HEADINGLY + NILE + LANCASHIRE FARM & handing over demolition stores for Bridges 4 & 3 to 297 field Coy RE. Lt McLEAN still i/c work for T.M.s & R.F.A.	
"	19		as for 18th	
"	20th		O.C. at Brigade HQ fresh instructions re sector received by Brigade. Visit Canal bank E & NILE with Brigadier & horse lines with Capt Russell. Conference at 124 men with Brigadier CRE & OC 124. North limit of Coy area SKIPTON & including Bridge & E side of canal. J Wood Major RE	

WAR DIARY or INTELLIGENCE SUMMARY

Army Form C. 2118

123rd FIELD COMPANY ROYAL ENGINEERS.

Place	Date	Hour	Summary of Events and Information	Remarks and references to Appendices
YPRES CANAL BANK E. side near Bridge 3b.	21/4/17		Major Wood proceeded to Horse Lines. Captain Russell visited work at NILE, LANCASHIRE FARM and EAST CANAL BANK, NORTH of Bridge 4.	
	22nd		Major Wood proceeded on leave. Captain Russell temporarily assumed command. Acting O.C. visited all work in progress.	
	23rd		As for 22nd instant.	
	24th		Visited work with Lieut McLean at A.121 Battery and R.A. work with Lieut Kent has shared supervision for JOY FUSE FARM. Reconnoitred with Lieut Kent tramway to FRONT LINE. GLIMPSE COT. tramway to 227th Field Company R.E. Visited work on EAST CANAL BANK.	
	25th		Started new work at HILLTOP to 227th Field Company R.E. Visit to all work in progress. Marked out proposed tramway of trench from Bridge 6 x to through Horse Lines to C.2.a.6.8. (Sheet 2C)	

62 All Russell Capt. A.D.S.S.

…

WAR DIARY or INTELLIGENCE SUMMARY

123rd FIELD COMPANY ROYAL ENGINEERS

Army Form C. 2118

Place	Date	Hour	Summary of Events and Information	Remarks and references to Appendices
YPRES. CANAL BANK. E. side near Bridge 3.b.	26th April 1917.		Acting O.C. visited work in progress.	
	27th		Conference at Bn. H.Q. re working parties. Lieut. E. William, R. Banks, C. Stocks re reinforcements with 15th Welsh Regt. H. Rounsfell for aerial work with 15th Welsh Regt. Visit to work in progress on EAST Canal Bank. Instruction re Demolition party detailed in various days to 15th Welsh Regt. from 11.30 am to 12-40 pm. (144 men detailed by 1/24 of 3 W.L. Coy. NCOs to 13th Welsh Regt also attended) by Captain Russell. R.E. Captain Russell attended Machine Gun Farm in connection with proposed demolitions.	
	28th		Visit to 114th Brigade and 13th Welsh Regt re forthcoming operations by Captain Russell. Instruction to 1 C.O. then of 123rd 9, 13+ 5+ 3.0 Coy on demolitions for forthcoming operation by Captain Russell. Lieut. J. Phillib subaltern for H. Davies (on arrival of 26th Kemel). Visit to Horse Lines by Captain Russell. (A.O.C.)	
	29th		A.O.C. visited work in progress at Isle Lance. Farm and East Canal Bank. Instr. to 1 C.O. then re demolition charges for forthcoming raid.	

WAR DIARY
or
INTELLIGENCE SUMMARY

Army Form C. 2118

128rd FIELD COMPANY ROYAL ENGINEERS.

Place	Date	Hour	Summary of Events and Information	Remarks and references to Appendices
YPRES CANAL BANK E. side near Bridge B.6.	29th	9pm	The following 1. C.O. Sappers handing at Coy. HQ. to assist in raid on MORTELDJE SALIENT with 13th Welch Regt. — No. 62593 Lance Corpl. F. WHITTINGTON, No. 108036 Sapper W.E.F. WILLIAMS, No. 62595, Sapper E. WILLIAMS, No. 62407, Sapper W.J. BOND, No. 146711, Sapper R. BANKS, No. 108030, Sapper J. PHILLIPS, No. 140709, Sapper S.B. STOCKER, No. 95749, Sapper W.F. WENHAM. The party remained in enemy trenches 45 minutes and demolished various structures i.e. Machine Gun Emplacements, Dugouts, Snipers Posts and Blockhout Shelters. On returning about 1-15 am night of 29th/30th No 62407. Sapper W.J. BOND sustained a gunshot wound (slight). A/o.C. visited work in progress on EAST CANAL BANK. Various supports to Canal Bank by foot animals.	MAP REFERENCE SHEET ST JULIEN. C.15.
	30th			

J. Russell Catrice
128rd FIELD COMPANY
ROYAL ENGINEERS.

Secret Vol 18

Original War Diary

May — 1917.

123rd Field Company R.E.

31-5-1917

Army Form C. 2118

WAR DIARY
or
INTELLIGENCE SUMMARY

123rd Field Coy R.E.

May 1917

Place	Date	Hour	Summary of Events and Information	Remarks and references to Appendices
YPRES. CANAL BANK. E.side near BRIDGE 3.b.	1/5/17.		No 1 Section 2/Lieut. DICKINSON. Work at Chris's Yard & 39 Dugouts. No II " 2/Lieut. SOUTAR. " on CANAL BANK, EAST. No III " " EVANS " Tram lines between CONEY STREET and SKIPTON ROAD. Coy H.Q. at NILE, LANCASHIRE FARM and HUDDERSFIELD. No IV Section 2/Lieut Floyd. Work at 42 defences under VIII Corps.	
	2nd "		O/C. visited work in progress on Canal Bank, Chris Danks and Nile. A/o.C. visited work on tram lines, Nile, Lancs Farm & Canal Bank. Company "Stood too" by Dugout for GAS ALARM from 10-15 p.m. to 10-35 p.m. 1 Attached Infantry (Pte Walby, 15th Welsh) wounded at C.a. 3.6. at 10-15 p.m.	
	3rd "		A/o.C. visited work on CANAL BANK and Horse Lines at PËSËTHOEK. A.D.S.S. visited work at NILE and Tramway Q. GAS ALARM at 11-20 p.m. Company "Stood To". Company then on account recited.	

Army Form C. 2118

WAR DIARY
or
INTELLIGENCE SUMMARY
(Erase heading not required.)

Instructions regarding War Diaries and Intelligence Summaries are contained in F. S. Regs., Part II. and the Staff Manual respectively. Title Pages will be prepared in manuscript.

Place	Date	Hour	Summary of Events and Information	Remarks and references to Appendices
YPRES.	4/6/17		A/O.C. visited work on CANAL BANK and Rk. Dumps, also work in tile, Lancashire Farm and all knowways.	
CANAL BANK E. side near BRIDGE 3.b.	5/6/17		A/O.C. visited Horse Lines "Back Billets" with Lt. Loulor.	
	6/5/17		—"— work on CANAL BANK.	
			A/O.C. visited work on CANAL BANK, HUDDERSFIELD, NILE, LANCASHIRE FARM and all knowways. Inspected Dumps at RAILWAY COTTAGE and AUSTERLITZ. CANAL BANK heavily shelled.	
	7/6/17		A/O.C. visited work on CANAL BANK & HUDDERSFIELD and Dumps. Visit to Horse Lines. Horse hit on picket lines. Musketry practice for sections on CANAL BANK.	
	8/5/17		A/O.C. accompanied G.O.C. Bng Gen'l 118th Infy, G.S.O.I. & R.E. round Left Divl Sector and that of Right Sector. Musketry practice.	
	9/5/17		A/O.C. visited work on CANAL BANK & Dumps & FRONT LINE. CANAL BANK shelled heavily.	
	10/6/17		Visited work on CANAL BANK, DUMPS & DUMPS. Musketry practice. CANAL BANK shelled heavily family.	
			Major J. I. Wood R.E. returned from leave & resumed Command.	

1875 Wt. W593/826 1,000,000 4/15 J.B.C. & A. A.D.S.S./Forms/C. 2118.

Army Form C. 2118

WAR DIARY
or
INTELLIGENCE SUMMARY
(Erase heading not required.)

Instructions regarding War Diaries and Intelligence Summaries are contained in F. S. Regs., Part II. and the Staff Manual respectively. Title Pages will be prepared in manuscript.

Place	Date	Hour	Summary of Events and Information	Remarks and references to Appendices
YPRES Canal Bank E side near Bridge 3b.	11/5/17		Capt RUSSELL visited work in hand on canal bank E, tramways NLLE, LANCASHIRE Fm., MIRFIELD. also Brigade H.Q. in dugouts No 4 section. room was found in tunnel dugouts in canal bank W.	weather fine + warm waterlevel very low in canal
	12/5/17		No 4 Section marched in. Preparing plantation & proposed causeway	
	13/5/17		No 4 section improving accommodation remainder as on 11/5.	
	14/5/17		No 4 Section take over "Canal Bank East" North of Bridge 4 making dugouts 5.9 proof. remainder as on 12th	
	15/5/17		"	
	16/5/17		as on 13th.	

rain.

Army Form C. 2118

WAR DIARY
or
INTELLIGENCE SUMMARY
(Erase heading not required.)

Instructions regarding War Diaries and Intelligence Summaries are contained in F. S. Regs., Part II. and the Staff Manual respectively. Title Pages will be prepared in manuscript.

Place	Date	Hour	Summary of Events and Information	Remarks and references to Appendices
YPRES	17/5/17		OC + Capt Russell visit all works in hand	rain
E Bank of YSER CANAL near Bridge 3b			No 2 Section Lt SOUTAR Canal Bank E Dugouts in Bs 6 Tramlines, Cy H 6m NILE + MIRFIELD	
			No 3 Section Lt EVANS	
			No 4 Section "Lt LLOYD Canal Bank E 5.9 proofing dugouts N. of Bs 4	
"	18/		worked on 17 Ft.	fine
	19/		OC + Capt Russell visit horse lines + infant teams Brigade change 114 relieves 113 two squads of NCO + 10 men to horse lines for instruction in pipe pushing with Sentinel Jack	fine warm
"	20/		Start work on embankment at Brg for one day Two more squads on Sentinel Jack.	hot
"	21/		" OC + Lt Evans to horse lines instruct pipe pushing squad + arrange for Sentinel Jack etc to be sent up to front line by train + tram.	

Army Form C. 2118

WAR DIARY
or
INTELLIGENCE SUMMARY
(Erase heading not required.)

Instructions regarding War Diaries and Intelligence Summaries are contained in F. S. Regs., Part II. and the Staff Manual respectively. Title Pages will be prepared in manuscript.

Place	Date	Hour	Summary of Events and Information	Remarks and references to Appendices
YPRES E Bank of YSER CANAL near Bridge 3b	22/6/17		GC + ST EVAN'S visit all work in hand and Batt line re proposed new work as on 17th. Steady rain.	Two men wounded by shell fire.
	23	Am	CRE visited Canal Bank + work on causeway at Br 5 with OC	
		11pm	weather fine. CRE visited front line + posts 28 to 22 re new trenches	
	24th		St Evans laid out new trenches with steamjam rehearsed by day + night of parties for night work (behind and) new trenches dug by 15th Welch Regt under supervision of St Evans. C.T.s from posts 23 and 26 being dug by attached infantry. No casualties except on wiring which was carried out later. Steamjam laid out for support line St Julien	
	25th	11pm		
	26th	11pm	Support line from St Julien road to Butt 17 dug by 15th Welch. No casualties. an 15th Welch	
	27th	4pm	Batt change C.T.s laid out in steamjam from top of Huddenfield to Post 23 and SE of PILCHEM Rd to Post 17	

Army Form C. 2118

WAR DIARY
or
INTELLIGENCE SUMMARY

(Erase heading not required.)

Instructions regarding War Diaries and Intelligence Summaries are contained in F.S. Regs., Part II. and the Staff Manual respectively. Title Pages will be prepared in manuscript.

Place	Date	Hour	Summary of Events and Information	Remarks and references to Appendices
YPRES E Bank of YSER Canal near Bridge 3b	28/5/17	11 pm	CTs dug by 18th & 14th Welsh under supervision of 2/Ls Evans and Lloyd. Coy returned by 1.51. Field Coy march to Noval lines advance party to WATTEN	
	29/5/17	8.45	Coy entrain at POPERINGHE & proceed to WATTEN. Mounted section & Transport to ZEGGERS CAPPELL	
Billets in WATTEN	30/5/17		Coy doing infantry drill & physical exercise. reconnaissance of bricks for "Tanks". WATTEN See Ch Asting 2/Lt MORRIS S/C presented with "Medaille Militaire"	
	31/5/17		Constructing bridge for Tanks. Urgent repair of Barge bridge	

J Wood Major RE
OC 123 Fd Co RE

Secret

Original

War Diary – June 1917

123rd – Field Coy. Royal Engineers

38th (Welsh) Division.

30-7-1916.

WAR DIARY
or
INTELLIGENCE SUMMARY

(Erase heading not required.)

Army Form C. 2118

123 Field Coy R.E.

Place	Date	Hour	Summary of Events and Information	Remarks and references to Appendices
WATTEN	1.6.17	6am	all sections Physical Training	
		7:30am	" " unpacking & packing tool carts × Nos 1 & 2 sections cutting experimental causeway for tanks — making water jumps & do. & blowing shell holes	
			" " Extended order drill	
			" " Semaphore signalling	
"	2	6am	Physical training	
"	3	9am	Ch. Parade	
			Tanks arrive	
"	4	6am	Physical training	
		7.50	entraining & hustling & lashing	
			Car for 4.4	
"	5		Tanks proceed to Trial ground test satisfactory 2 – 4 pm	
		5pm	Sports meeting	
		7.30pm	Concert on canal bank	

WAR DIARY or INTELLIGENCE SUMMARY

Army Form C. 2118

(Erase heading not required.)

Instructions regarding War Diaries and Intelligence Summaries are contained in F. S. Regs., Part II and the Staff Manual respectively. Title Pages will be prepared in manuscript.

Place	Date	Hour	Summary of Events and Information	Remarks and references to Appendices
WATTEN	6.6.17	6am	all Sections Physical Training	
		7.30am	(knotting & lashing)	
		9am	1 & 4 Musketry (firing)	
			2 & 3 Pontooning	
	7.6.17	as for 6th	1 & 4 Pontooning	
			2 & 3 Demolitions	
			ex cept Nº 3 demolishing causeway etc.	
	8.6.17	9am	" inspection of R.E. san appliances	
			Coy parade	
			Nº 4 dismantling causeway stitching up	
	9.6.17	5am	reveille	
		6am	Physical drill	
		7.30am	Nºs 1 & 2 Paulin's Pontoons	
			all inf to Nº 3 knotting lashing & demolitions	

> Army Form C. 2118

WAR DIARY
or
INTELLIGENCE SUMMARY
(Erase heading not required.)

Instructions regarding War Diaries and Intelligence Summaries are contained in F.S. Regs., Part II. and the Staff Manual respectively. Title Pages will be prepared in manuscript.

Place	Date	Hour	Summary of Events and Information	Remarks and references to Appendices
WATTEN	10.6.17	9am	Church parade	
		2.30pm	Church parade	
	11.6.17	6am	Physical Training	
		7.30am	Sections overhauling + packing transport	
		2pm	Transport to ZEGGERS CAPPEL under 2/Lt McLEAN awaiting Lt LLOYD	
WATTEN	12.6.17	6am	Physical Training	
		7.30	at disposal of Sections On.	
			OC + advanced party to CARDOEN also Transport to CARDOEN	
	13.6.17	"	To Canal Bank take over billets work from oc 124 Fd.Co.R.E. Transport at CARDOEN Sections + off. Inf. by road + STOMER Train to POPERINGHE & road to Canal Bank via MOUTON Fm. CRE visits trenches with oc 124 + oc 173	
CANAL BANK N of Bn Hd N of YPRES			+ right flank until oc 151 also site for new Causeway	

Army Form C. 2118

WAR DIARY
or
INTELLIGENCE SUMMARY
(Erase heading not required.)

Instructions regarding War Diaries and Intelligence Summaries are contained in F. S. Regs., Part II. and the Staff Manual respectively. Title Pages will be prepared in manuscript.

Place	Date	Hour	Summary of Events and Information	Remarks and references to Appendices
N. of YPRES	14.6.17	am	No 1 Section ("Lt DICKENSON) FARGATE + Front line + 2/o 1 OCT	weather fine
N of B'h on YSER CANAL			Lt DICKENSON) WR. CRK.	fine & HOT
			No 2 Section Lt SOUTAR C.T. through SZWAANHOF F'm	
			No 3 Section Lt EVANS Canal bank work "Bally" dugouts main entr'ys etc.	
			No 4 Section Lt LLOYD Front line "	
	15	7h	attached infantry raided East bank of Canal + cleared 125 coy dugout. Canal bank shelled	
		3am	worked on 14th Thick Mist in morning so visited all work in hand including new Trenches	
"	16	pm	Lt Dickenson rejoined Coy. Canal bank shelled	More lines in wood E of VOXVRIE
		3am	work as on 15th	
		11am	OC to Horse lines + Q camp. Lt EVANS to bank areas on leave from 15th	
		9	Canal bank shelled	
		1pm	Shared mess of officers dugouts with 151 Fd Coy who moved into dugout between Br 5 + 6	
"	17	3am	work as on 16th on selecting site for dumps at AUSTERLITZ + BELMONT being	
		am	visit from GOC + CRE. investigating cause of stoppage of water in 9" pipe	
			Suffer W. N. LEWIS killed & L Cpl E MORGAN wounded by shell fire	
			Whilst repairing foot bridge over YSER CANAL	

WAR DIARY
or
INTELLIGENCE SUMMARY

(Erase heading not required.)

Army Form C. 2118

Place	Date	Hour	Summary of Events and Information	Remarks and references to Appendices
YSER CANAL W Bank N of YPRES	18/6/17		Casualty Pte H.F. GALE attached from 13th WELSH Inft. KILLED by shell fire also Pte. ISAK DAVIES. Lights at Coy HdQrs.	1 OR wounded at duty 1 O.A. wounded
"	19/		2nd Lt. DOYLE rejoined this unit from Base	
"	20/		Arrival at MARENGO HOUSE convoy of casualties 17th & 18th Bz4998	
"	21/		Worked as on 14th. Lt DOYLE Taking over No 3 section.	

Army Form C. 2118

WAR DIARY
or
INTELLIGENCE SUMMARY

(Erase heading not required.)

Instructions regarding War Diaries and Intelligence Summaries are contained in F. S. Regs., Part II. and the Staff Manual respectively. Title Pages will be prepared in manuscript.

Place	Date	Hour	Summary of Events and Information	Remarks and references to Appendices
YSER CANAL W BANK N. of YPRES	22		Work as on 14th.	
"	23		Casualties 1 O.R. wounded at duty (Coy #2) 3 " " (New Trench)	
"	24		Casualties 1 O.R. wounded 1 " " at duty	
"	25		sitting dugout in ALMA trench with Lt. WHITE 17th RWF. Bridge 6 W damaged by shell fire, repaired & tramway made good. Pipe cut in YPERLEE often to Brigade H.Q. I some of ours dropped slightly overnight §.4.2. Digging new trench E of trench, near Lt. of HUDDLESTON ROAD this morning	

Army Form C. 2118

WAR DIARY
or
INTELLIGENCE SUMMARY
(Erase heading not required.)

Instructions regarding War Diaries and Intelligence Summaries are contained in F. S. Regs., Part II. and the Staff Manual respectively. Title Pages will be prepared in manuscript.

Place	Date	Hour	Summary of Events and Information	Remarks and references to Appendices
YSER CANAL W BANK N of YPRES	27/6/17		Work as usual	
"	28		Visit from CRE's 29th & 38th Divs. Casualties 1 OR wounded 2 killed C.19.a.2.1. Mounting parties from 2/ormy & Div Cllry	thunder
"	29		29th Division relieve 38th. 143 Coy left behind to carry on work. 151 & PROVEN & HERZEELE Conference with CRE 29th Div at 87th Brig. HQ or visits horse lines & back billets	fine
"	30		Casualties 1 all ofr killed & = YORKSHIRE TR (77 men) 1 h " wounded	rain

J. Woolfhayo Col.
CRE 1st 3rd Div S.S.

SECRET

Original

War Diary – July 1917.

183 Field Co Royal Engineers
38 (Welsh) Division

1-8-1917.

Vol 20

WAR DIARY
or
INTELLIGENCE SUMMARY

(Erase heading not required.)

Army Form C.

123rd FIELD COMPANY
ROYAL ENGINEERS.

Instructions regarding War Diaries and Intelligence Summaries are contained in F.S. Regs., Part II. and the Staff Manual respectively. Title Pages will be prepared in manuscript.

123 Field Coy R.E.

Place	Date	Hour	Summary of Events and Information	Remarks and references to Appendices
YSER CANAL W BANK N of YPRES between Bridge 4 + " 5	1-7-1917		No 1 Section making new front line HARVEY TRENCH + BAIRD EXTENSION (CT10) Lt DICKINSON	
			No 2 Section making MOAT Trench through S. ZWAANHOF Lt SOUTAR (Tchakbills?) Dugouts in WELSH HARP (handing over to Lt DOYLE) Tunnels in W Canal Bank	
			No 3 Section Maintaining Tramways (Windsor castle line) Lt DOYLE R.E.T. Dugouts in W Canal Bank (handing over to Lt EVANS) Drawing stores, water supply, etc.	
			No 4 Section making new front line HARVEY TRENCH + HARWICH Lt LLOYD Dugouts in WHITE + ALMA	
			O.C. to C.R.E. 29th with O.C. 29th Div Pioneers + O.C. Kent R.E.T Field Coy (Monmouth)	
			Via ONDANK DUMP Train from onbank	C.7.C.1.6.
"	2/7/17		Work as on 1st. O.C.4 Lt DOYLE reconnoitre gun road from YPRES - BOESINGHE Rd 5am to canal bank & over sap at Post 41 + report on same to C.R.E.	
			4pm Lt Dickinson reports to Brigade re stores for infantry work on front line trenches + " Lt Lloyd to O.C. R. & S. Bn. for " "	

Army Form C. 2118

WAR DIARY
or
INTELLIGENCE SUMMARY
(Erase heading not required.)

123rd FIELD COMPANY ROYAL ENGINEERS.

Instructions regarding War Diaries and Intelligence Summaries are contained in F. S. Regs., Part II. and the Staff Manual respectively. Title Pages will be prepared in manuscript.

Place	Date	Hour	Summary of Events and Information	Remarks and references to Appendices
			123 Field Coy RE	
YSER CANAL W.BANK	3.7.17		Work as for 1st + 2nd.	
	8			
"	9.7.17		Shell burst in cookhouse in Canal Bank killing two men wounding 3 (section cooks + cookmate) (12ShroBank billets)	
			Bean in G. Camp also hit some 3 casualties among labour Pers.	
"	10.7.17		Work as for 1st + 2nd.	
"	11.7.17		Capt. 29th Div. visit work with OC.	
"	12.7.17		Work as on 1st	
"	13.7.17		10 Reinforcements from Base	
"	18		"	
"	19		Lt SOUTAR slightly wounded (at duty)	
"	20		38th Div relieve 29th.	
"	21		Coy relieved by 151 Field Coy in SZWAANHOF FARM SECTOR	
			123 returned to G.Camp relating No1 Section to HOUTKERQUE taking over tents of 151	
G.Camp	22		No 2 Section to HOUTKERQUE	
"	23		& No 1 Section to G. Camp Aug 3rd.	Sheet 28
	24		Coy moved to Bivouacs in Wood opposite Dragon Camp near Houseshie	

WAR DIARY or INTELLIGENCE SUMMARY

Army Form C. 2118

128th FIELD COMPANY ROYAL ENGINEERS

123 Field Coy R.E.

Place	Date	Hour	Summary of Events and Information	Remarks and references to Appendices
DRAGON CAMP WOOD	25/7/17		Resting	
"	26		Making cellar gas proof at adv Div Hd, ELVERDINGHE	
"	27		Lt Doyle R.S.T. transferred to 151 Fd Coy R.E. No 4 Section to HOUTKERQUE No 2 returning to "Camp Horselim"	
"	28		No 3 & 4 Sections reform unit at H.Q.s Standing by prepared to move at ½ hrs notice. ½ hr notice cancelled.	
"	29		Standing by. 15 men working at Ordank	
"	30	10 pm	Transport moved up to advanced horse lines nr "Bridge Junction" south of ELVERDINGHE CHATEAU	
"	31st	3:50 am	Zero on 2 day move from G Camp via No 9 track + horse lines to Canal Bank reporting to C.R.E. at ELVERDINGHE CHATEAU at 5 am. On arrival at CANAL BANK shortly after 6 am. moved to GREEN LINE + consolidated it detailed report follows. Casualties 2 OR killed 3 OR wounded J.C.J.Wood Major R.E. or 123 Fd Coy R.E. 3 attached infantry OR wounded.	

SECRET

Vol 21

Original War Diary.

123rd Field Company,

Royal Engineers – 38th (Welch)

Division

August 1917.

1-9-17

WAR DIARY or INTELLIGENCE SUMMARY

Army Form C. 2118

123rd FIELD COMPANY ROYAL ENGINEERS.

123rd Field Coy. R.E.

Place	Date	Hour	Summary of Events and Information	Remarks and references to Appendices
Canal Bank N of YPRES	1/8/17		Coy. in Reserve resting.	
"	2	4 am	No 1 Section collecting tools ready for extension of GLIMPSE COTTAGE Tramline. Stevens reconnoitring line.	
		10 am	3rd 4th Sections extending GLIMPSE COTTAGE tramline & repairing existing parts. 19th Welsh Pioneers assisting.	
		12 noon	124 Infantry Bgde. 1st & 2nd Sections carrying CRE decides to push tramline on instead of round by PILCKEM ROAD.	
"	3		On as for 2nd. Got line laid in the two days.	
"	4		On for 2nd. Line through to PILCKEM ROAD near 5 CHEMINS 2 attached infantry O.R. wounded.	
"	5		On for good. Also leaving PILCKEM ROAD (infantry working parts) & laying trench grids beyond opposite GALLWITZ farm finishing up with 6 W Bridge with switch on GLIMPSE COTTAGE line. Spr. JONES E.S. wounded.	

WAR DIARY or INTELLIGENCE SUMMARY

Army Form C. 2118

128rd FIELD COMPANY ROYAL ENGINEERS.

Place	Date	Hour	Summary of Events and Information	Remarks and references to Appendices
CARDOEN FARM	6/8/17	6-7pm	Move to CARDOEN FARM from Canal Bank, hand over 83rd Fd Coy. & commenced work on Bank Bank Road	
	7 8 9 10 11	12-7pm	along HUDDLESTON RD. 3rd Section up to 10pts & sett. inform to hospital & 17-2 as above, from in own ride Sugar 19 Welsh Pioneers return on 13th by 13th Welsh. Also 2.0 blidges 20 noticeboards	
	12 13 14 15		weather variable, went heavy thunderstorms 16th Sec & attring to hospital 12 H DONE from 151 7d Coy at Road through to GUARDS area on left 2nd Lt GRIFFITHS from Base 20 haggs return to 153 Field Re	
	16 17 18		No movement 20th Div's attacking LANGEMARCK Shown of WELSH FARM for Ork.	
	19		Lt SOUTAR R2 to 124 Field Coy R.E.	
HQ Nr.249 Section B.23.central	20 21		No 3 Section on mule track along STADEN Railway beyond STEENBEEK. In dressing Body at crossing of mule track on STEENBEEK repairing CACTUS pontoon Bridge 14 of ONDANK dump again in field at CARDIEN FARM HQ Nr.24.93 & other (on 3 sector) founded the 14th Section of ONDANK R Nr 2 erecting shelters presented etc. In 3 or 4 mls track	

Army Form C. 2118

WAR DIARY
or
INTELLIGENCE SUMMARY
(Erase heading not required.)

128rd FIELD COMPANY ROYAL ENGINEERS.

Instructions regarding War Diaries and Intelligence Summaries are contained in F. S. Regs., Part II. and the Staff Manual respectively. Title Pages will be prepared in manuscript.

Place	Date	Hour	Summary of Events and Information	Remarks and references to Appendices
Bivouac B.29 Central	2.2		Nos 3 & 4 Sections changed round. Nos 2 & 1 CARDOEN Farm to 23 central.	
Nr YPRES with Inspections at	2.3		Nos 2 & 4 Sections on track & C.T. Nos 1 & 3 off. Spr. Evans V (No 3 Section) wounded.	
CARDOEN FARM working at	2.4		Nos 2, 3 & 4 Sections on track & C.T. Lt. DOYLE & Evans to C.R.S. injuries from buried mine etc	
R.E. Dump ON BANK homeline W. of	2.5		Nos 2 & 4 Sections on track & C.T.	
DAWSON'S CORNER	2.6		Nos 2 & 1 Sections changed round.	
"	2.7		Nos 1 & 4 Sections on mule track to STEENBEEK & C.T. South of DAVIES ST. Overnight awning to protective operation. Steady rain	
"	2.8		No 1 Section under Lt GRIFFITHS & No 4 Section under Lt LLOYD consolidating U.25.d.4. Lt. 57. Capt McLEAN 1/C proceeded to STRAY FARM in advance for instructions while Coy took cover in CANAL BANK order having come through to move up (though the infantry had not taken the cemetery (this objective) the action proceeded to the site which was practically in the outpost line. No 1 had two casualties. Sgt. Mason Killed Wilson wounded. No 1 & 4 CARDOEN to rest & dry. No 3 to 23 central	

1875 Wt. W.593/826 1,000,000 4/15 J.B.C. & A. A.D.S.S./Forms/C. 2118.

Army Form C. 2118

WAR DIARY
or
INTELLIGENCE SUMMARY
(Erase heading not required.)

128rd FIELD COMPANY
ROYAL ENGINEERS.

Instructions regarding War Diaries and Intelligence Summaries are contained in F. S. Regs., Part II. and the Staff Manual respectively. Title Pages will be prepared in manuscript.

Place	Date	Hour	Summary of Events and Information	Remarks and references to Appendices
HQ & 3 sections B 2 3 central	29/8/17		Two sections laying duckboard track from MACKEM road near IRONCROSS to LANGEMARCK Stn. No 4 Section at ONDANK	
	30		Three sections duckboarding track near IRON CROSS No 4 Section at ONDANK CRE + OC visit green line in front of LANGEMARCK	
	31st		No 3 section taking duckboards to IRON CROSS – LANGEMARCK Stn track Two sections digging green line in front of LANGEMARCK. No canals. No 4 section at ONDANK.	

J. Wood Major RE
OC 128 Fd Coy RE

1875 Wt. W593/826 1,000,000 4/15 J.B.C. & A. A.D.S.S./Forms/C. 2118.

Secret.

Original War Diary

September 1917.

123rd Field Co. Royal Engineers.

38th (Welch) Division.

1. 10. 1917

Army Form C. 2118

WAR DIARY
or
INTELLIGENCE SUMMARY
(Erase heading not required.)

123rd FIELD COMPANY
ROYAL ENGINEERS.

Place	Date	Hour	Summary of Events and Information	Remarks and references to Appendices
H.Q. N. 3 Sections at B. 23 Central	1/9/17	6.30 pm	Nos. 1 & 2 Sections Digging Trenches (Support Line) Excavation line 387' × 3' × 3' No. 3 Section Carrying Trenchboards No. 4 Section "ONDANK"	U.23.C.5.4 & U.23.C.73 C.3.a.1.3. to U.27.d.4.8
	2/9/17		Nos. 2 & 4 Sections Digging Trenches (Support Line) U.29. & 10.95. No. 1 Sect "ONDANK" No. 3 Sect Organising Carrying Trenchboards & Shell holes at L.2. (Experiments) from C.5.a.1.3 to U.27.d.4.8	U.23.C.91. U.23.C.85.00
	3/9/17		Nos. 2 & 4 Sections Digging Trenches (Support Line) U.29.6.2.7 & U.29.6.3.5 & U.29.6.4.9. Work was very much delayed by Heavy barrage of H.E. & gas shells. No. 3 Section Organising Shellholes at L.2 No. 1 Section "ONDANK" Coy Wood Carr Company to be a C.R.E. 38 Div. Capt Horton took command of Company	U.27.d.4.8 U.29.b.2.7 & U.29.b.3.5
	4/9/17		Nos. 3 & 4 Section Digging Trenches No. 2 Section Organising Shellholes at L.2. No. 1 Section "ONDANK" Capt Horton proceeds on leave, leaving Major Boyle in command of Company.	U.29.a.9.5.

Army Form C. 2118

WAR DIARY
or
INTELLIGENCE SUMMARY
(Erase heading not required.)

123rd FIELD COMPANY
ROYAL ENGINEERS.

Instructions regarding War Diaries and Intelligence Summaries are contained in F.S. Regs., Part II. and the Staff Manual respectively. Title Pages will be prepared in manuscript.

Place	Date	Hour	Summary of Events and Information	Remarks and references to Appendices
H.Q. & 3 Sections at B.23 Central	5/9/17		O.C. Company & Sergt Price & two Sappers attend funeral of late C.R.E. 32 Div. (Lt Col Philpotts) who died from wounds received in action.	
	2/9/17		Lt T Oakley-Jones joined unit from Base.	
			No 4 Section. Organising Shell holes at L.2.	
			No 1 Section. ONDANK	
			No 3 & 2 Section. Digging Trenches (support line) Parties could not get to work owing to intense Barrage with H.E. & Gas shells.	
H.Q. & 3 Sections at B.23 Central	6/9/17		No 2 Section. Carrying material and building Artillery bridge across the STEENBEEK at (B1) 28.d.25.40. Bridge complete.	
			No 4 Section. Digging Trenches (support line) the Trench system as laid down by Reasons was completed.	
			No 3 Section. relieved No 1 Section at ONDANK	
			No 1 Section. to B 23 Central then resting.	
			A reconnaissance of all Bridges in Divisional sector was made & report sent in to C.R.E.	
			Camps shelled with 8" H.E.	
	7/9/17		Company moves to "CARDOAN FARM" leaving details at B. 23 Central. Lt Evans to 151 Field Coy. 60 2nd in Command.	

Army Form C. 2118

WAR DIARY
or
INTELLIGENCE SUMMARY

(Erase heading not required.)

128rd FIELD COMPANY
ROYAL ENGINEERS.

Instructions regarding War Diaries and Intelligence Summaries are contained in F. S. Regs., Part II. and the Staff Manual respectively. Title Pages will be prepared in manuscript.

Place	Date	Hour	Summary of Events and Information	Remarks and references to Appendices
GARDOEN FARM.	8/9/17		No 3 Section "ONDANK" Remainder overhauling tools, Bridging Equipment etc. Major abroad R.E. returns to Unit from being Act. C.R.E. Major & Lt/Col T.E. KELSALL having taken over duties of C.R.E.	
"	9/9/17		No 3 Section ONDANK remainder clearing the STEENBEEK and strengthening bridges & fixing wheel guides	
"	10/9/17	8:30 am	109 hrs the Section SALEM camp near CROMBECK with 113 group. March to No 3 section march in after work at ONDANK	
SALEM camp. near CROMBECK	11/9/17		resting + cleaning up generally	
"	12/9/17	7:30 11.0 am	route march of all dismounted men by sections (9 miles) visit from C.R.E. + adjt.	2"

1875 W^t. W593/826 1,000,000 4/15 J.B.C. & A. A.D.S.S./Forms/C. 2118.

Army Form C. 2118

WAR DIARY
or
INTELLIGENCE SUMMARY
(Erase heading not required.)

128rd FIELD COMPANY
ROYAL ENGINEERS.

Instructions regarding War Diaries and Intelligence Summaries are contained in F. S. Regs., Part II. and the Staff Manual respectively. Title Pages will be prepared in manuscript.

Place	Date	Hour	Summary of Events and Information	Remarks and references to Appendices
ERQUINGHEM	18/9/17		Work on Drainage & Roads in Bois Grenier & Chap. D'Armentière sectors. also maintenance of C.T.s & construction of T.M. emplts. etc. Visit Bn HQ & Bn HQrs	
"	19/9/17		" Lt LLOYD No 4 Section on night Fm Greenwood av to Moat Farm incl. " Lt GRIFFITHS " ind Shaftsbury av Tramway Av & Park Posn No 3 " av ind Shaftesbury av	
"	20/9/17		Lt DOYLE No 2 Sec next Wellington av Haystack av & Nine av.	
"	21/9/17		" Dickinson No 1 Sec on Left ind. Cowgate & Leithwalk	
"	22/9/17		Conference at Bn HQ Visit Bn HQrs Visit Shaftesbury av & Moat Fm av & Top of Greenwood av	

1875   W: W593/826   1,000,000   4/15   J.B.C. & A.   A.D.S.S./Forms/C. 2118.

Army Form C. 2118

WAR DIARY
or
INTELLIGENCE SUMMARY
(Erase heading not required.)

123rd FIELD COMPANY
ROYAL ENGINEERS.

Place	Date	Hour	Summary of Events and Information	Remarks and references to Appendices
SALEM Camp near CROMBEEK	13/9/17		6 mile route march in morning. Baths 3 miles away & took from 1½ to 2 miles	
" to EEKE	14/9/17		March with 113 Brigade halt for dinner near WATTOU fine	
" to MORBEKE	15/9/17		March with 113 Brigade	"
" to ESTAIRES	16/9/17		"	"
" to ERQUINGHAM	17/9/17		March to billets took over billets from 505 Fd Co R.E.	"

Army Form C. 2118

WAR DIARY
or
INTELLIGENCE SUMMARY
(Erase heading not required.)

128rd FIELD COMPANY ROYAL ENGINEERS.

Instructions regarding War Diaries and Intelligence Summaries are contained in F.S. Regs., Part II. and the Staff Manual respectively. Title Pages will be prepared in manuscript.

Place	Date	Hour	Summary of Events and Information	Remarks and references to Appendices
ERAVINGHAM	23/9/17		Sunday. Church parade – rest day pm football match v Sussex Coy we win 7–0.	weather fine
"	24/9/17		Reconnaissance of Rue Fleurie, Rue Marle & GHQ 2nd line for C.R.E.	calm mist morning fine hot later
"	25/9/17		Inspect Drainage, with C.R.E. also junction with RUE FLEURIE Switch, Windygates dump, R.A.P. SHAFTSBURY AV. MOAT FARM AV. WHITE CITY H.T.M. emps. GREATWOOD AV. MG dugouts etc. To Brigade, thence office	
"	26/9/17		Inspect NEW FARM for MG emplacement meet Tramway officer & arrange meeting with Brig. Gen. 113 Brigade	
"	27/9/17		measure up NEW FARM etc with Dr GRIFFITHS Meet Br.G. Rf Bn meet Tramway officer re extension of GREATWOOD tramway & go with him to Brigade	

1875 Wt. W593/826 1,000,000 4/15 J.B.C. & A. A.D.S.S./Forms/C.2118.

WAR DIARY or INTELLIGENCE SUMMARY

128rd FIELD COMPANY ROYAL ENGINEERS.

Army Form C. 2118

Place	Date	Hour	Summary of Events and Information	Remarks and references to Appendices
ERQUINGHEM	28/9/17		Lt GRIFFITHS No 3 section on back area work under adjt. No 2 & 4 Sections to take over work of No 3 in line. O.C. sick.	Weather fine
"	29/9/17		Lt Lloyd on leave. Working parts table to Brigade. Visit from C.R.E. to O.C. (Office work only) reports etc.	"
"	30/9/17		Sunday church parade. Inspection of BAC ST MAUR Bridge (No1 Section acct Lt DICKINSON). Office work diary reports files etc.	

J Wood Major RE
O.C. 123 Fd Co RE
30.9.17

Army Form C. 2118

WAR DIARY
or
INTELLIGENCE SUMMARY

(Erase heading not required.)

123rd FIELD COMPANY ROYAL ENGINEERS.

Vol 23

Instructions regarding War Diaries and Intelligence Summaries are contained in F.S. Regs., Part II. and the Staff Manual respectively. Title Pages will be prepared in manuscript.

Place	Date	Hour	Summary of Events and Information	Remarks and references to Appendices
ERQUINGHEM LAUNDRY	1/10/17		No 1 Section in left section area under 2Lt DICKINSON	
"			No 2 Section in left centre " Lt DOYLE	
"			No 3 Section on back work under 1 Lt GRIFFITHS under ADJT. R.E.	
"			No 4 Section in right Bn area under Lt DAMAN	
"	2/10/17	9.45 am	Met C.R.E. at WINDY FLATS DUMP with G.S.O.1. & D.M.G.O. selected sites for M.G. with 1 Lt DAMAN & set out revised sketches for M.Gs at NEW F.M. & OVEN	
"	3/10/17		weather for 1st	
"	4/10/17		"	
"	5/10/17		Visits down from CROMBAHOT to LAIE BLANCHE D'ERQUINGHEM	
"	6/10/17	8 am	Meet Br Gen P.D. at Bn H.Q. & go round Brigade area from WHITE CITY SAFETY ALLEY - STANWAY AV. Top of SHAFTSBURY AV. RUE DU BOIS SALOP F.M. DE BIEZ LEITH WALK - COWGATE L.DN. H.Q. Work on on 15 T.	
"	7/10/17		Sunday. Rest day.	

Army Form C. 2118

WAR DIARY
or
INTELLIGENCE SUMMARY
(Erase heading not required.)

128rd FIELD COMPANY
ROYAL ENGINEERS.

Instructions regarding War Diaries and Intelligence Summaries are contained in F.S. Regs., Part II. and the Staff Manual respectively. Title Pages will be prepared in manuscript.

Place	Date	Hour	Summary of Events and Information	Remarks and references to Appendices
ERQUINGHEM LAUNDRY	8/10/17	10 am	Work as on 1st. Visit groups HQs & go round pills etc. Long hopeless wait for flash screening.	fine
"	9/10/17		Work as on 1st. Visit OPs with Lt DICKINSON & work in his sector. C.R.E. also there but did not meet.	
"	10/10/17		Work as on 1st.	
"	11/10/17	9.30 am	C.R.E. visits 6"TM emp. with O.C. & D.T.M.O. also main drains & KEITHWALK, COWGATE WINE AV. PARK ROW & TRAMWAY AV. M.G. emp.	fine
"	12/10/17	11 am	O.C. at 13th R.W.F. Bn HQ. re Summary of Evidence in case of no 176/15 Pte D. Williams Lt LLOYD returning from leave. Lt DAMAN superintending No 3 Section Royal Sa. Brigade Conference. Visit wiring YESEE SWITCH. TRAMWAY AV. emp. & demolition charges.	pm wet
"	13/10/17	9.30 pm	CROMBAJGT. R.A.P. SHAFTESBURY AV. BOIS GRENIER water supply etc. Work as on 12th.	fine rain later
"	14/10/17		Sunday. Rest day. 2 pm football match. V. Signals lost 1 to 2.	fine
"	15/10/17		Ride to BAILLEUL with Lt Lloyd (road past WATERLANDS) visit from Capt McKEAN & later Capt SOUTAR re transfer of attached R.W.F. Office. Work crew on 12th.	fine

1875 Wt. W593/826 1,000,000 4/15 J.B.C. & A. A.D.S.S./Forms/C. 2118.

Army Form C. 2118

WAR DIARY or **INTELLIGENCE SUMMARY**
(Erase heading not required.)

123rd FIELD COMPANY ROYAL ENGINEERS.

Instructions regarding War Diaries and Intelligence Summaries are contained in F.S. Regs., Part II. and the Staff Manual respectively. Title Pages will be prepared in manuscript.

Place	Date	Hour	Summary of Events and Information	Remarks and references to Appendices
ERQUINGHEM LAUNDRY	16/10/17	9.30 am	Work as on 12th. Brigade Conference. O.C. visits Beacon O.P. Moat Fm. WHITE CITY Brewery H.T.M. BUCKINGHAM GATE SAFETY ALLEY TUI Rd. STANWAY AV. R.A.P. SHAFTSBURY AV. (GRIS POT shelled)	
"	17/10/17		Office. Lt DOYLE to BAC ST. MAUR re stores (Bac St Maur Dump shelled)	
"	18/10/17	9.30 am	706255 L/Cpl E. DAVIES wounded. Work as on 12th. Brigade Conference. (SAPPER DOYLE) 10.30 O.R. witness at F.G.C.M. 15th R.W.F. No 6255 L/Cpl E. DAVIES died of wounds	
"	19/10/17		Work as on 12th	
"	20/10/17	9.30 am	Conference. Work as on 13th. Attached inf transferred with those of 124 under Lt G. WILLIAM 15th R.W.F.	
"	21/10/17		Sunday. Rest day. O.C. to STEENWERK STN re Trench Tramways at left Bn. also searched for hospitals. P.M. to Divl. H.Q. re Screwing.	

WAR DIARY or INTELLIGENCE SUMMARY

Army Form C. 2118

123rd FIELD COMPANY ROYAL ENGINEERS

Place	Date	Hour	Summary of Events and Information	Remarks and references to Appendices
ERQUINGHEM LAUNDRY	22/10/17		See Br. Gen. & O.C. R.A. Group re changes along with Lt DOYLE ride up emergency roads to front, inspect work in Rt Bn area. Work as on 19th attached(ing) to roads draining & screening	Air mail
"	23/10/17		O.C. sick (gastritis) Lt DOYLE to conference. Work as on 19th (C.R.E.'s visit)	
"	24/10/17		O.C. still in bed. Work as on 19th	
"	25/10/17		Conference postponed. Work as on 19th	
"	26/10/17	9.30	Brigade Conference. Lt DOYLE to attend. Work as on 19th	
"	27/10/17		Visit from C.R.E. Work as on 19th	
"	28/10/17		Sunday. Rest day. Loy. flag a 122 R.F.A. v win. 2 goals to 1. at CROIX DU BAC. O.C. visits Brigade & R.A. Group H.Q.	

WAR DIARY

Army Form C. 2118

123rd FIELD COMPANY ROYAL ENGINEERS

Place	Date	Hour	Summary of Events and Information	Remarks and references to Appendices
ERQUINGHEM LAUNDRY	29/10/17		Visit Brigade + R.A. Group H.Q. re Platoon O.P.s Visit Ave Charles - Cromboust Subsidiary line trophole & defence of C.T. M.G. emps. of Oven & New Fm & Tramway A.K inspect drainage generally & roads about LAVESSE. Work as on 27 ½.	fine
"	30/10/17	930	Brigade Conference at DOYLE attended. Afternoon Captain McKEAN returns to Coy. from Div R.E. H.Q. Work as on 12½.	stormy
"	31/10/17		O.C. + Capt. McKEAN visit works in Rt. Bn. Brigade H.Q. R.A. Centre Group H.Q., R.A.P. (New Farm), "2nd tube gunpits", emergency road, M.G. emps. at Oven + NEW FARM. WINDYGATES dump, TRAMWAY AV. camouflage M.G. emp. Bn. H.Q. see gun tried in loophole at Oven, SHAFTSBURY AV. R.A.P. baby elephant shelter for Lewis gunners a top of " TUI Rd., H.T.M. Brewery GREATWOOD AV CROMBAUT dump, BEACON O.P. Pumping Stn at Brewery BOIS GRENIER & Roads & drains in area returning via emergency road & GRIS POT pm inspect Horselines with Capt. McKEAN. Work as on 12th	fine

J.J. Ford Major R.E.
O.C. 123 FM Coy R.E.

Secret.

Original
War Diary. Novr 1917

123 Field Coy. R.E.
38 (Welsh) Division.

2-12-1917.

WAR DIARY
or
INTELLIGENCE SUMMARY

Army Form C. 2118

Place	Date	Hour	Summary of Events and Information	Remarks and references to Appendices
ERQUINGHEM LAUNDRY	1/11/17		OC & Capt. McLEAN visit left Bn. area via L'ARMEE, LA VESEE Bn. H.Q. Meet Lt. DICKINSON visit ORCHARD via HAYSTACK ALLY, QUEEN ST, then PARADISE ALLEY For DU BIEZ. Inf dugout near LEITH WALK + 6" TM emp, LEITH WALK dump GLENFIELD O.P., SCOTCH H.Q. O.P. WYNE ST dump. Inf dugout in WELLINGTON AV returning via RUE MARLE/Midscreening through ARMENTIERES to office	fine

Army Form C. 2118

WAR DIARY
or
INTELLIGENCE SUMMARY
(Erase heading not required.)

Place	Date	Hour	Summary of Events and Information	Remarks and references to Appendices
ERQUINGHEM LAUNDRY.	2/11/17		Lt Doyle went to Brigade Conference in the morning. Capt McKean inspected the forward dumps.	
	3/11/17		Visits R.E. / Ops in left battl. with Lt Stevenson.	
	4/11/17.		Patrolled with Lt Doyle all drainage from Corps boundary to front line in left sub sector. It was noted that Conveau de la Chapel requires widening & cleaning in sq. I. 15.a. Sappers were detailed for preparing & fixing bangalore torpedoes on the enemy's wire near INCH TRENCH.	
	5/11/17.			

Place	Date	Hour	Summary of Events and Information	Remarks and references to Appendices
ERQUINGHEM LAUNDRY.	6/10/17		Demonstration for blowing up Kangaloons was carried out before G.O.C. 113 Inf Bde. Major F.C.L. Wood left the Company on leave.	
	7/10/17		Capt. McKean temporarily took over Command of Company.	
	8/10/17		On the night of the 7-8th 6 Kangaloons Torpedoes were blown up successfully by Sapper F. Pottery and Spr. G. F. Jones. Raid by 115 Inf. Bde on the left proved very successful - 14 Prisoners Captured	

Army Form C. 2118

WAR DIARY
or
INTELLIGENCE SUMMARY
(Erase heading not required.)

Place	Date	Hour	Summary of Events and Information	Remarks and references to Appendices
ERQUINGHEM. LAUNDRY.	9/14/17		Visited work in left sector.	
	10/14/17		" " in the after noon.	
	11/14/17		Conference at Bn HQrs. The question of Stores for forward dumps was gone into thoroughly and orders were handed to each Section Officer, C.S.M. and N.C.O.s prepared for the 113 Inf. Bde. to be	
	12/14/17		kept near the enemy's wire - two Sappers detailed for laying the charge.	
	13/14/17		Reconnoitered new KEITH WALK tramway with S.T.O. - 5 Bridges to be constructed.	
	14/14/17		Conference at Bde HQrs. with reference to H.M Engels - Heavy & Medium.	

WAR DIARY or INTELLIGENCE SUMMARY

Place: ERQUINGHEM LAUNDRY

Date	Hour	Summary of Events and Information	Remarks and references to Appendices
15/10/17		Bridges for New LEITH WALK TRAMWAY commenced.	
16/10/17		Conference at Bn. HQrs in Rubert Line. The CRE went into the question of the demolition of bridges & the Pontoon Bridge with Capt McLean and it was decided that the present scheme for destroying BAC-ST. MAUR & ERQUINGHEM BRIDGES was not satisfactory. Capt. MCLEAN was told to go into the matter and prepare new schemes.	
17/10/17		Received orders about moving from present billets to JUTE FACTORY ARMENTIERES.	

Army Form C. 2118

WAR DIARY
or
INTELLIGENCE SUMMARY
(Erase heading not required.)

Place	Date	Hour	Summary of Events and Information	Remarks and references to Appendices
ERQUINGHEM LAUNDRY.	18/11/17.		Inspected the new billets at the TUTE FACTORY and arranged full details with the Section Officers as to the distribution of the men. Two Sappers were detailed from each section to do the work.	
	19/11/17.		Brigade Conference at Rk. Bn. Hqrs. Land mine fires in the enemy's wire. Made arrangement with G.O.C. for erecting new Bn. Hqrs. at I.19.c.4.8.	
	20/11/17.		Spr. D. M. Richards 82588 killed at Ely Farm. I.19.c.80.60.	

WAR DIARY or INTELLIGENCE SUMMARY

Army Form C. 2118

Place: ERQUINGHEM LAUNDRY

Date	Hour	Summary of Events and Information	Remarks
21/10/17		Coy. moved into new Billets at the JUTE FACTORY ARMENTIERES. returned back from Major J.C. Loos leave.	
22	930	Capt McLEAN to Conference at office reading up filth stats. Visited right Bn area with Capt McLEAN & Lt DAMIAN	
23		Visited left Bn area with Lt DICKINSON	
24		Sunday rest day. No 3 section to billets opposite Rt Yard ERQUINGHEM remainder of Coy marching order	
25		11am inspection by O.C. visited C.R.E. at CROIX du BAC	

WAR DIARY
INTELLIGENCE SUMMARY

Army Form C. 2118

Place	Date	Hour	Summary of Events and Information	Remarks and references to Appendices
JUTE FACTORY ARMENTIERES	26/11/17	9.30 am	OC to Conference at Rt Bn HQ. Visited work in Rt Bn area. New snipers Hars. New Bn Hars M.G. emplacement.	heavy T.M. fire on STANNAY POST.
	26/11/17	pm	Central drainage system down {DYKES, DYKE 3, Brickfield Stream} w/o branch drains draining DESCRANGE Fm area. Emergency tracks & screening in front of RUE MAARLE met GOC + CRE, & returned via O+ U1 tanks	
	27/11/17		OC visited emergency routes & work in Rt & Left Bn areas with Lt DOYLE	rain
	27/11/17	pm	visited Centre group R.A.H.Qs & Brigade on return.	T.M. firing on KNIGHTS BRIDGE
	28/11/17		New 200 yds firing Range commenced for 113 Inf Bde.	

Army Form C. 2118

WAR DIARY
or
INTELLIGENCE SUMMARY

(Erase heading not required.)

Instructions regarding War Diaries and Intelligence Summaries are contained in F. S. Regs., Part II. and the Staff Manual respectively. Title Pages will be prepared in manuscript.

Place	Date	Hour	Summary of Events and Information	Remarks and references to Appendices
JUTE FACTORY	29/11/17		Made arrangement for Emergency forward Dumps.	
ARMENTIERES	30/11/17		O.C. went round HOPLINES AREA with C.R.E. and O.C. 151. Field Coy.	

M. J. Cooper Lt.
23.12.17
O. C. 1 ? ?

1875 Wt. W593/826 1,000,000 4/15 J.B.C. & A. A.D.S.S./Forms/C. 2118.

<u>Secret.</u>

Original War Diary — January 1918

123 Field Comp.y, Royal Engineers
38th (Welsh) Division

1-2-1918

Secret

Original

War Diary – December 1917.

123rd Field Co. Royal Engineers

1-1-1918

WAR DIARY
or
INTELLIGENCE SUMMARY

(Erase heading not required.)

Army Form C. 2118

123rd FIELD COMPANY
ROYAL ENGINEERS.

Place: JUTE FACTORY ARMENTIERES

Date	Hour	Summary of Events and Information	Remarks and references to Appendices
1/12/17		O.C. at Hqrs. Acting C.R.E. CAPT. McLEAN took over Command of Coy.	
2/12/17		Sunday. Concert held in the evening to celebrate the 2nd Anniversary of the Coy. coming overseas. - Great success.	
3/12/17		Conference at R.E. Batt. Hqrs.	
4/12/17		Heavy P.M. Enfd. near Brewery Completed.	
5/12/17		Work on new Coy. Hqrs at I.15.c.70.45.	

Army Form C. 2118

WAR DIARY
or
INTELLIGENCE SUMMARY
(Erase heading not required.)

123rd FIELD COMPANY ROYAL ENGINEERS.

Instructions regarding War Diaries and Intelligence Summaries are contained in F. S. Regs., Part II. and the Staff Manual respectively. Title Pages will be prepared in manuscript.

Place	Date	Hour	Summary of Events and Information	Remarks and references to Appendices
JUTE FACTORY. ARMENTIERES.	6/10/17		Conference at Br. Batt. Hqrs.	
	7/10/17		New forward Baths at "QUATRE CHEMINS" completed.	
	8/10/17		Lt. Sortie of the 124 A.S. Inf. arrived at these billets with one section, as an advanced party to prepare new billets for the 124 Coy.	
	9/10/17		Sunday.	
	10/10/17		Interview with C.R.E. reference O.P.s.	MW

WAR DIARY
or
INTELLIGENCE SUMMARY
(Erase heading not required.)

Army Form C. 2118

123rd FIELD COMPANY
ROYAL ENGINEERS.

Place	Date	Hour	Summary of Events and Information	Remarks and references to Appendices
JUTE FACTORY ARMENTIERES	11/10/17.		Visited CULVERT FARM with C.R.E. and arranged details on the site for making into a Strong Point.	
	12/10/17.		Visited new R.A.P.; new Coy Hqrs. Orchard Foot Baths (been present from Bois Store) and inspected new Screens along RUE FLEURIE and arranged details with O.C.Pavilion on the site.	
	13/10/17.		Conference at Rt: Battl. Hqrs.	
	14/10/17.		Visited CULVERT FARM.	

WAR DIARY or **INTELLIGENCE SUMMARY**

Army Form C. 2118

123rd FIELD COMPANY ROYAL ENGINEERS.

Place	Date	Hour	Summary of Events and Information	Remarks and references to Appendices
JUTE FACTORY ARMENTIERES.	15/12/17		BEACON OP: & "GIRLS SCHOOL" completed. New Cnj. Sgrs.?	
	16/12/17		Sunday.	
	17/12/17		Conference at R. Bath. Hqrs. 124 Cnj. R.E. moved into new Billets. Bois GRENIER water supply line again out of action owing to frost. Repairs being carried out.	
	18/12/17		Notification received to move Billets	
	19/12/17		Standing over work to 11th Australian Field Cnj. From LEITH WALK to PARK ROW Communication Trench.	

Army Form C. 2118

WAR DIARY
or
INTELLIGENCE SUMMARY

123rd FIELD COMPANY
ROYAL ENGINEERS.

(Erase heading not required.)

Instructions regarding War Diaries and Intelligence Summaries are contained in F. S. Regs., Part II. and the Staff Manual respectively. Title Pages will be prepared in manuscript.

Place	Date	Hour	Summary of Events and Information	Remarks and references to Appendices
G.17.a.9.2. Sheet 36.	20/10/17		Coy. moved from JUTE FACTORY to new billets at G.17.a.9.2. Sections 2 & 4 carried on with the work in the Rept. & Centre sectors.	
	21/10/17		Nos. 1, 2 & 4 Sections on work in the line. Attached Infantry employed at R.S. Park.	
	22/10/17		DO.	
	23/10/17		Sunday - the Coy. soccer team played 124th Field Coy. RE.	
	24/10/17		Conference at Brewery, BOIS GRENIER.	

WAR DIARY
INTELLIGENCE SUMMARY

123rd FIELD COMPANY ROYAL ENGINEERS.

Army Form C. 2118

Place	Date	Hour	Summary of Events and Information	Remarks and references to Appendices
Sheet 36. G.17.a.9.c.	25/12/17		Xmas day. Coy. Soccer & Rugby teams played in the morning and afternoon. Turkeys issued to the men a great success! All working parties supplied by Bde were cancelled.	
DO	26/12/17		Nos 1, 2 & 4 on works. Attached infantry on repair of roads.	
DO	27/12/17		Made out scheme of drainage for ABBOTS TRENCH AND BAY AVENUE. 1 - 2 Sappers detailed to report to Coys in the line to assist with the work.	
DO	28/12/17		Slender MOAT FARM with Bde Major re new Batt. H.qrs.	GWM

WAR DIARY — 128rd FIELD COMPANY ROYAL ENGINEERS — Army Form C. 2118

Place	Date	Hour	Summary of Events and Information	Remarks and references to Appendices
Sheet 36. G.17.a.9.2.	29/12/17.		Coy. moved into New Billets at FORT ROMPU.	
FORT ROMPU.	30/12/17.		Sunday. Party of Sappers detailed to work on New Horse lines under 2nd Griffith	
Do.	31/12/17.		Inspected all Concrete Pillboxes (Pill-boxes) in course of erection in the Line with C.R.E. Coy. held a Concert in the Evening.	

Geoff R Clarke Capt R.E.
a/O.C. 128rd FIELD COMPANY ROYAL ENGINEERS.

Army Form C. 2118

WAR DIARY
or
INTELLIGENCE SUMMARY
(Erase heading not required.)

123rd FIELD COMPANY
ROYAL ENGINEERS.

123   Vol 26

Place	Date	Hour	Summary of Events and Information	Remarks and references to Appendices
FORT ROMPU	1/1/18.		Inspected new Horselines with C.R.E. - Frost still continuing - Concrete work held up.	
Do	2/1/18		Frost still continuing	
Do	3/1/18.		Inspected new billets at "RUE DORMOIRE". Went over billets and only accommodation for 100 men	
Do	4/1/18.		Frost still continuing	
Do	5/1/18.		Capt McLean attended Court of Enquiry at ERQUINGHEM regarding loss by fire of FARM BUILDINGS in RUE DU MOULIN	

WAR DIARY

123rd FIELD COMPANY ROYAL ENGINEERS.

Place	Date	Hour	Summary of Events and Information	Remarks and references to Appendices
FORT ROMPU	6/1/18		Coy. Transport lines moved to new lines at LA BOUDRELLE - work on the new stonelined was not completed.	
do.	7/1/18		Major Hood returned from H.qrs and took over command of the Company.	
"	8/1/18		Got out plans for Brigade Battle H.Q.	
"	9/1/18		Take over pontoon bridges nos 5 + 6 from 124 Alloy	
"	10/1/18		Plans of Brigade Battle H.Q. back from C.R.E. also lists of details of Inf + R.A. to be accommodated at Brigade Battle H.Q.	
"	11/1/18		Start work on Brigade Battle HQ, clearing guardroom S.W.	

Army Form C. 2118

WAR DIARY
or
INTELLIGENCE SUMMARY
(Erase heading not required.)

123rd FIELD COMPANY
ROYAL ENGINEERS.

Instructions regarding War Diaries and Intelligence Summaries are contained in F. S. Regs., Part II. and the Staff Manual respectively. Title Pages will be prepared in manuscript.

Place	Date	Hour	Summary of Events and Information	Remarks and references to Appendices
Fort ROMPU	12/1/18	2 pm	Moved to Brigade School Rue DORMOIRE. Work in line as usual	
RUE DORMOIRE	13/1/18		Sunday no day. Visit from OC 69th Fd Coy to re work & billets Visit proposed billets near Fort ROMPU	Snow
" move to old horse lines near FORT ROMPU	14/1/18		Move to billets near Fort ROMPU handing over work to OC 69th Fd Coy R.E.	
	15/1/18		Visit work & billets of 69th Fd Coy R.E.	Thaw
Mon T LA HAYE Fm.	16/1/18		Commence work under XV Corps on concrete MG shelters wiring & trenches from #22 to #18 central	

J.W.

Army Form C. 2118

WAR DIARY
or
INTELLIGENCE SUMMARY

128rd FIELD COMPANY
ROYAL ENGINEERS.

(Erase heading not required.)

Place	Date	Hour	Summary of Events and Information	Remarks and references to Appendices
LA HAYE FARM	17/1/18		Working under XV Corps on concrete MG Emp shelters. River rising rapidly, sand at wharf under water during shelling	
PONT DE NIEPPE	18/1/18		work as for 17th. Approaches to bridges flooded	
"	19/1/18		work as for 17	
"	20/1/18		Sunday. Rest day (owing to shortage of stores)	
"	21/1/18		work as for 17th	
"	22/1/18		"	
"	23/1/18		"	Fine
"	24/1/18	6am	Thaw. Precautions off. Resume normal traffic.	Fine Fine

WAR DIARY
or
INTELLIGENCE SUMMARY

Army Form C. 2118

128rd FIELD COMPANY
ROYAL ENGINEERS.

(Erase heading not required.)

Instructions regarding War Diaries and Intelligence Summaries are contained in F.S. Regs., Part II. and the Staff Manual respectively. Title Pages will be prepared in manuscript.

Place	Date	Hour	Summary of Events and Information	Remarks and references to Appendices
LA HAYE FARM	25/1/18		C.E. & CRE Corps troops visit works, spitlocking trenches & mixing, first concrete shelter complete	
"	26/1/18		start concrete work at CANTEEN FARM, spitlocking, mixing	
"	27/1/18		Sunday. Cox team beat D 1.2.1 by 2 goals to love of course fixing reinforcement in floor of concrete shelter	
"	28/1/18		finish concrete in floor	
"	29/1/18		erected small steel shelters, digging trenches, one bath, wump Cpl Ruggles representing Divl RE beat RA & TM HQ 2 goals & true, Phil visit from CRE	
"	28/1/18		work as for 29th	
"	31/1/18		intersection, soccer match no 4 methods no 4 methods by 3 goals to love V Wood Major RE OC 128 3d Inf Bde

1875 Wt. W593/826 1,000,000 4/15 I.R.C. & A. A.D.S.S./Forms/C. 2118.

Army Form C. 2118

WAR DIARY
or
INTELLIGENCE SUMMARY
(Erase heading not required.)

Vol 27

123 Field Coy R.E.

Place	Date	Hour	Summary of Events and Information	Remarks and references to Appendices
LA HAYE FARM near PONT DE NIEPPE	1/2/18		Constructing reinforced concrete dugouts under C.R.E. XV Corps Troops. No 1 Section under 2nd Lt DICKINSON at CANTEEN FARM. 4 ft of reinforced concrete one 25 small steel shelters 21 ft long each. Material transported by lorry to Farm, thence	
	2/2/18		by tip trucks on decauville to site, hence traction being used and the trucks run up on both sides of the work. Two mixing boards were used and two shifts a day completed this job on the 3rd.	
"	3/2/18		Remainder of Coy collecting material & preparing site and widening 2nd Lt DAMAN on leave 3rd to 17th	
"	2/2/18		Played 2nd round Soccer Div tournament, beaten by 3 D.A.C. 4 goals to 3	
"	3/2/18		Played 2nd round Rugby Div tournament beat D.A.C. 11 pts to nil	
"	6/2/18		No 2 Section under Lt DOYLE started reinforced Concrete Dugout at STREAKY BACON FARM working three shifts a day two mixing boards on site and one at Farm. Tip trucks with graded decauville and horse haulage by block & tackle up to both sides of work being employed. Concrete completed in 4½ days	
"	8/2/18		Capt McLEAN returns from G.H.Q. R.E. Sch. of Inst.	J.W.

Army Form C. 2118

WAR DIARY
or
INTELLIGENCE SUMMARY
(Erase heading not required.)

Instructions regarding War Diaries and Intelligence Summaries are contained in F.S. Regs., Part II. and the Staff Manual respectively. Title Pages will be prepared in manuscript.

Place	Date	Hour	Summary of Events and Information	Remarks and references to Appendices
LA HAYE FARM near PONT DE NIEPPE	9/2/18	12.15 pm	No 3 section work, in preparation for No 4 dugout, hit by shell falling short during bombardment of gun positions (vacated recently) no casualties as men were withdrawn in time.	
"	10/2/18		No 3 dugout completed by No 2 section.	
"	11/2/18		Lt. L.L.OYD on leave to PARIS till 18th. Trilogy. Officers & Sgts. beat 151st 3 pts to nil. at Rugger.	
"	12/2/18		Non section beat No 1 section 3 goals to nil. at Soccer.	
PONT DE NIEPPE	15/2/18	10am	Coy. relieved 505 Field Coy. in the ARMENTIÈRES sector and took over billets at PONT DE NIEPPE with Horselines in huts at → B28b5.1 and handed over work under XV Corps to 505 field coy. No 3 section under Lt GRIFFITHS took over work in line with 113 Brigade & billets near SACRE COEUR CHURCH.	B23c5530

J.W.

Army Form C. 2118

WAR DIARY
or
~~INTELLIGENCE SUMMARY~~

(Erase heading not required.)

Instructions regarding War Diaries and Intelligence Summaries are contained in F. S. Regs., Part II. and the Staff Manual respectively. Title Pages will be prepared in manuscript.

Place	Date	Hour	Summary of Events and Information	Remarks and references to Appendices
PONT DE NIEPPE	21/2/18	11 am	Visit proposed work with C.R.E. in ASYLUM & FERME DES JARDINS LOCALITIES	
"	22/2/18	10 am	do a/o.c Pioneers	
"	23/2/18 23/2/18		(Capt. McLEAN on leave till 9/3/18) do with Corks Cr. XV Corps	
"	25/2/18	2:30 pm	Won Group Final of Rugby Div. Tournament v R.A.M.C. 6 pts to 3 pts.	
"		7 pm	3 coys 16th R.W.F. working on posts in ASYLUM & FERME DES JARDINS LOCALITIES	
"	26/2/18	7 pm	do.	
"	28/2/18		Visit work with C.R.E.	

J. Woof Major R/k
O.C. 123 2/London R

Secret.

Original War Diary - March 1918

123 Field Company, Royal Engineers

38 (Welch) Division

1-4-1918

WAR DIARY
or
INTELLIGENCE SUMMARY
(Erase heading not required.)

Army Form C. 2118

123rd FIELD COMPANY
ROYAL ENGINEERS.

123 Field Coy RE

WE 28

Place	Date	Hour	Summary of Events and Information	Remarks and references to Appendices
PONT DE NIEPPE	1/3/18		No 3 Section under Lt GRIFFITHS working under 113 Brigade in the Centre Sector "ARMENTIERES"	
"	2/3/18		No 1 Section under 2/Lt DICKINSON preparing cellar at SANDBAG CORNER for concealing also wiring & superintending infantry digging trenches in "WAARMEE" line along with Nos 2 & 4 Sections from RUE HAVES to BUTERNE Lane 1 Coy 19th Welch Rowe also working in this sector	
"	3/3/18		"CARDIFF"	
"	4/3/18		No 2 Section also working on O.P. near Railway Stn ARMENTIERES and on "VICTORY" aid post near SANDBAG CORNER 1 under Lt DAMANT	
"	5/3/18			
"	6/3/18			
	7/3/18			
	8/3/18			
	9/3/18		Major WOOD to Div HQ to take over from C.R.E. Capt McKEAN returned from leave	
	10/3/18		Sunday	JW

Army Form C. 2118

123rd FIELD COMPANY
ROYAL ENGINEERS.

WAR DIARY
or
INTELLIGENCE SUMMARY
(Erase heading not required.)

Instructions regarding War Diaries and Intelligence Summaries are contained in F. S. Regs., Part II. and the Staff Manual respectively. Title Pages will be prepared in manuscript.

Place	Date	Hour	Summary of Events and Information	Remarks and references to Appendices
PONT DE NIEPPE	11/3/18		Major Wood (O.C. Coy) at Div Hqrs. acting C.R.E.	
"	12/3/18		Capt McEwan took over Command of Company. Mr Dickinson on leave till 25th to England. Inspected work on new trenches &c with C.R.E.	
"	13/3/18		Inspected site for new O.Ps in Armentières	
"	14/3/18		Met Adj R.S. at JESUS FARM. I went into the question of extending the accommodation in the existing Baths.	
"	15/3/18		Loading Parties supplied by 16th Batt. very much reduced - work on new Trench consequently very slow.	JW

1875. Wt. W593/826 1,000,000 4/15 J.B.C. & A. A.D.S.S./Forms/C. 2118.

WAR DIARY or INTELLIGENCE SUMMARY

Army Form C. 2118
128th FIELD COMPANY ROYAL ENGINEERS.

Place	Date	Hour	Summary of Events and Information	Remarks and references to Appendices
PONT DE NIEPPE	16/3/16		In a raid carried out by the 16th Battl. R.W.F. 12 Sappers were detailed to destroy concrete dugouts in the enemy's front support line. 2 Concrete D.O. were destroyed in the front line owing to the wire entanglements in rear of the enemy's front line it was not possible to reach the enemy's 2nd line. All the Sappers carried out their tasks very excellently and were greatly praised for their determination in the operation. Names of Sappers — Party No. 1 Sappers E. Lotley and J. Clyffe. Party No. M.G.D.S. Sappers C. Morris & B. A. Llewellyn. Party No. M.G.D. 2. L/Cpl. J. Milburn & Sapper Jacques. Party No. C.P. 2. L/Cpl. W. F. Sale & Sapper R. Blakefield? E. V. Davies & A. R. Bradley? Party Sub B2. Sappers W.? R. Jones, J. J. Rees 15/3 Prenler?, J. Hughes, Gunn?, J. Machell?	

Result of Raid —

WAR DIARY
or
INTELLIGENCE SUMMARY

(Erase heading not required.)

Army Form C. 2118

128rd FIELD COMPANY ROYAL ENGINEERS.

Place	Date	Hour	Summary of Events and Information	Remarks and references to Appendices
PONT DE NIEPPE	17/3/18.		2n/Cpl. S.E. Morris & party slightly gassed on their way to work in Armentières. ERQUINGHEM shelled by the enemy.	
"	18/3/18.		Visited the work on defences in front ARMENTIERES. Working parties supplied by the 13th Battl. R.W.F. and were very much under strength. Explained to O.C. "C" Coy Engineers on the ground what work was to be done on the support line Subsidiary line & the Asylum Keep. Heavy shells by the enemy during the morning - many Gas shells fell around SAND BAG CORNER.	
"	19/3/18.		Rained during the day - new trenches quickly affected and in parts flooded.	J.W.

Army Form C. 2118

123rd FIELD COMPANY
ROYAL ENGINEERS.

WAR DIARY
or
INTELLIGENCE SUMMARY
(Erase heading not required.)

Instructions regarding War Diaries and Intelligence Summaries are contained in F. S. Regs., Part II. and the Staff Manual respectively. Title Pages will be prepared in manuscript.

Place	Date	Hour	Summary of Events and Information	Remarks and references to Appendices
PONT DE NIEPPE	20/3/18		Major Wood returned back to the Company from UK.	
"	21/3/18	7am	Hostile gas shelling of area generally during the night morning 12" & 12" HE. to DOULIEU & DAMAN. & Q.Rs. to AIRE (gaz) & platoon. AIRE shelled with 12" HE.	
		10 am	O.C. & Capt McClean carried out preliminary recon. and survey. Reconnaissance of River LYS for 4 footbridges between ERQUINGHEM (No 2) and Railway Bridge (No 4)	
"	22/3/18	noon	O.C. met Corps. Cr. at Bassin ARMENTIERES	
		1pm	CRE. handing over work North of Ferme des JARDINS to PIONEERS (19th Welch) Back areas shelled with 12.8? 17" shell [Flemtz] aux JUTE factory piece fell in approaches & killed	
"	22/3/18	7am	Lt WOOD on leave to England for 14 days. 12/3/18 5/4/18	
		7.30am	16 7th RWF. working in trenches in "L'ARMEE line No 1 section taking over work with 113 Brigade in line from No 3 section	
"	23/3/18	8am	Capt McClean to Corps Gas School for one day course	
	"		Lt DAMAN and 2 ORs to School of Infantry training for 5 weeks course to 27/4/18	
		10am	O.C. met a/adj at B.25.c.7.5. re new horse lines for 114 Inf Bng.	
"	24/3/18	9am	Major HOOD on 2 day course Corps Gas School. 24 - 26th	

J.W.

WAR DIARY
or
INTELLIGENCE SUMMARY

(Erase heading not required.)

128nd FIELD COMPANY
ROYAL ENGINEERS.

Army Form C. 2118

Place	Date	Hour	Summary of Events and Information	Remarks and references to Appendices
PONT DE NIEPPE	25/3/18		Major Wood returned from Gas School. (School closed)	
"	26/3/18		2. Lt DAMIAN returned from Infantry Course (School closed) wiring in front of intermediate zone & digging in front line & ditto. O.C. inspected work being taken over on M.G. shelters (concrete, cupola type) 2 Lt DICKINSON rejoined from leave	
"	27/3/16		14th Bn R.I.F. wiring in front of intermediate zone & digging support line of ditto. One section on cellar at Sandbag corner concreting walls.	
"	28/3/18		One section on M.G. shelter at M18 b 35.35 erecting camouflage hanging trade one 2 section on M.G. shelter at ?? entertaining infantry.	
"	29/3 18		Good Friday. Rest day. Inspection of sections, packing up spare kit etc. getting out handling over reports. (118 Brigade moved to DOUVIEU) Presentation of Distinguished Service Certificate to Major Gale & Milburn and Sappers Jones, Jacques, Savies & Cliffe by O.C.	
"	30/3 18		10 am march to Billet in DOUVIEU over at Le TROU BAYARD officers reconnaissance of MERVILLE ST, etc.	
LE TROU BAYARD	31/3/18			

38th Div.
V.Corps.

WAR DIARY

123rd FIELD COMPANY, R.E.

A P R I L

1 9 1 8

WAR DIARY
or
INTELLIGENCE SUMMARY
(Erase heading not required.)

123 Field Coy R.E.

Place	Date	Hour	Summary of Events and Information	Remarks and references to Appendices
TROU BAYARD MERVILLE	1/4/18	p.m.	March to MERVILLE Stn. & entrain complete with Transport in No 18 Train, leaving 10.5 pm	
MONDICOURT in train march to	2/4/18	10.30 pm 10 am	Detrain at MONDICOURT met by Lt. DICKINSON at Stn. March to TOUTENCOURT via PAS – MARIEUX – PUCHEVILLERS	
TOUTENCOURT	3/4/18		Billets in TOUTENCOURT very scarce, huts & hangar lent by the mill – horse lines near wood west of hangar.	
" to WARLOY	4/4/18	p.m.	March to WARLOY via CONTAY find billets for Coy + 151 in WARLOY good billets.	
"	5/4/18	9 am	S.O.R. wounded by shell fire. "green" Marking out & digging conference BAIZIEUX MILL to WARLOY-HEADAUVILLE road 20 sappers under CRE cover Troops remainder under CRE. trace ←21'→ ←31'→ 13"	
"	6/4/18		←5'→ 12" plan ←21'→ ←3'→ section Took 7 rmn rail light to dark WARLOY-HENENCOURT & WARLOY SENLIS road.	
"	7/"		19th Welsh Pioneers working between WARLOY-HENENCOURT & WARLOY SENLIS road	
"	8/"		& on Subtracks North of this. 4 sections 123 near HENENCOURT road	J.W.
"	9/"			
"	10/"			

WAR DIARY or INTELLIGENCE SUMMARY

123rd FIELD COMPANY, ROYAL ENGINEERS.

Army Form C. 2118

(Erase heading not required.)

Place	Date	Hour	Summary of Events and Information	Remarks and references to Appendices
WARLOY-BAILLON	10/4/18		At DOYAT & advance party. Table over work & Billets from 87th Field Coy. 12th Div.	
	11/4/18	2pm	4 sections & advanced H.Q. & attached Infantry march & billets near SENLIS in Bluff to north. O.C. visited Brigade H.Q. (morning same.) 123rd work inch 113 Big BIVOUAC near SENLIS Bluff W. of SENLIS	
SENLIS	12/4/18		work taken over "linking up support line running same.) 123rd work inch 113 Big Brigade working party. Table got out for work on dugouts for right, left, & reserve Bn. HQ.) advanced Brigade H.Q., Res Brigade HQ.) work also required on visual signal stn. at SENLIS Mill.	
"	13/4/18		Inspect wire on corps line north at Bn. HQ. 9 Bdt HQ. & proposed work at SENLIS Mill & adv. Brig HQ. with 2/Ld. LOPD find vents of old dugouts at battn. meet Brigadier Gen. 113 on site & arrange work.	
"	14/4/18		Inspect same in WARLOY with 2/GWILLIM & draughtsman C.R.E. requires surface plan, surface improved on plan of caves.	
"	15/4/18	10am	Horse lines & "battle surplus" move to CONTAY along with 124 + 15 Fd Coy. Billets poor, very crowded with troops. Dinner in "bivvies" 113 Rear	
"	16/4/18	10am	formed H.Q. & sections & attached move to V.15.b.28 near Brigade HQ. (sheet 57 DSE) & dig trenches for cover & erect shelters. Bluff N. of Senlis being outside W. of Div. area	

WAR DIARY
or
INTELLIGENCE SUMMARY — 123rd FIELD COMPANY ROYAL ENGINEERS.
(Erase heading not required.)

Instructions regarding War Diaries and Intelligence Summaries are contained in F.S. Regs., Part II. and the Staff Manual respectively. Title Pages will be prepared in manuscript.

Place	Date	Hour	Summary of Events and Information	Remarks and references to Appendices
SENLIS V.15.b.2.8 Sheet 57D S.E.	17/4/18	4.15 pm	Capt McLEAN + Lt DOYLE to Horse Lines along with Battle surplus. 2nd Lt LLOYD killed by rifle bullet. Sapper R BELL placed under arrest charged with murder of 2nd Lt LLOYD + marched to CONTAY for safe custody.	
"	18	11 am	Court of enquiry on Death of Lt LLOYD	
"	"	2.30 pm	Funeral of Lt LLOYD in WARLOY	
CONTAY	19 —	11 am	Summary of evidence for F.G.C.M. on Sp BELL taken	
SENLIS	20			
"	21		O.C. + Lt DAMAN to CONTAY with Battle Surplus. Saw M.G. Bn re M.G. emplacements in BAIZIEUX FORCEVILLE Line	
"	22		Visit site for M.G.s with Lt DAMAN 3 craters blown in roads at W.15.a.40.80 W.27.a.30.80 + W.21.c.85.70 (Sheet 57D SE)	
"	23		ordered to hand over to our Div + 124	J.W.

INTELLIGENCE SUMMARY

123rd FIELD COMPANY, ROYAL ENGINEERS.

(Erase heading not required.)

Place	Date	Hour	Summary of Events and Information	Remarks and references to Appendices
SENLIS	24		March to TOUTENCOURT, via CONTAY. Camped in wood (151 Fd Coy in huts in prisoners of war cage.)	
TOUTENCOURT	25	9am	Commence Training, Baths, drill etc.	
		2pm	Transport returned to CONTAY, sections to line (relief cancelled)	
SENLIS	26		Take over again from Aus. Div. R.E. & 124. Visit 115 Brigade H.Q. re work. Relief again ordered & the cmplete at 6am 27th hand over again to 124 + Aus Div R.E. Coy marches to TOUTENCOURT via CONTAY	
		7pm	Billets in TOUTENCOURT transport in old lines	
TOUTENCOURT	27	9-12am	Pontoon Trestle Bridging, squad drill, saluting, musketry, Box Respirators	
		2-4pm	drill. (Coy moved into huts + tents near 151 huts prisoners of war camp)	
"	28	9.30am	Sunday church parade. O.C. rode to DOULLENS with Lt DICKINSON	
		5.30pm	Officers + sgts. play officers + sgts. etc. of 151 at soccer 151 score one goal	
"	29		After from extra periods of training. Ground very slippery owing to rain	
		9-12noon	Drill + demolitions + platting (lashing (musketry, A.6.o Cmapreaching	
		2-4pm	C.R.E.'s visit to arrange visit Fline on 30th with O.C. Coy	
		6pm	Wrestling match (novitial) loxeback of (5-a-side) nos 1,2+3 sections v Hdqn nos 2 Kept no. 3. Held ns beat no 2.	Muir.
"	30	6am	Motor to HEDAUVILLE with C.R.E., Capt McLEAN + Capt EVANS (2nd in cd 151). Visit proposed work near MARTINSART. Coy. on musketry & rifle exercises ordered to relieve 203 Fd.Coy. 35 Div on 1st May	morning

J. Wood Major RE

Secret

Original War Diary

May 1918
———————

123 Field Coy Royal Engineers

38th (Welsh) Division.

1-6-1918

Army Form C. 2118

WAR DIARY
or
INTELLIGENCE SUMMARY
(Erase heading not required.)

128th FIELD COMPANY ROYAL ENGINEERS.

WO 30

Place	Date	Hour	Summary of Events and Information	Remarks and references to Appendices
TOUTENCOURT to V.8.a.7.7.	1.5.18	10 am	March to V.8.a.7.7. Sheet 57 D.S.E. Take over camp from 203 Fd Coy 35th Divn. & horse lines near HARPONVILLE. Move complete 2/pm. Officers visit 115 Brigade H.Q.S. S. of HEDAUVILLE. Nos 1 & 2 Sections for work under Brigade on C.T. along S. edge of MARTINSART WOOD and dugouts in HEDAUVILLE WOOD. at V.4.6.7.3. No. 3/4 Section for work under C.R.E. on PURPLE LINE trenches and wiring West of BOUZINCOURT.	
"	2.5.18		UPWILLING to hospital. work on dugouts in HEDAUVILLE WOOD stopped. 13th RWF. 2 dugouts as guard in ENGLEBELMER BOUZINCOURT line for two platoons (each) also double Bn. Hars. near W.7. central. on W.7.a.9.8. Later changed to W.7.b.4.9.	V.12.b & V.12.d
"	3.5.18		Selecting sites & getting out plans for dugouts as above	
"	4.5.18	2/pm	↑ work on dugouts at W.7.b.4.9.N.W. F.G.C.M. on Sapper R.BELL at CONTAY	W

Army Form C. 2118

WAR DIARY
or
INTELLIGENCE SUMMARY
(Erase heading not required.)

123rd FIELD COMPANY
ROYAL ENGINEERS.

Instructions regarding War Diaries and Intelligence Summaries are contained in F.S. Regs., Part II. and the Staff Manual respectively. Title Pages will be prepared in manuscript.

Place	Date	Hour	Summary of Events and Information	Remarks and references to Appendices
V8a 77 near MARTIN- -SART-MEDAUVILLE ROAD.	5/5/18		No. 166479 Spr. J BILLSBOROUGH wounded whilst attached to 16th R.W.F. Start work on dugouts in W.7.b.4.9. non section C.T. on edge of MARTINSART WOOD No. 2 Section work on PURPLE LINE under CRE. Nos. 3 & 4 Sections	
"	6/5/18		as before	
"	7/5/18		Blackelephants site for Bn. Dugouts with Brigade Major 113 Bn. W.7.b.3.7.	
"	8/5/18		Lt DOYLE to Battle Surplus. Lt MORGAN i/c No 2 section. No. 1 Section starts work on D.O. in W.7.b.3.7. which after two days work was taken over by 118 tunnelling Coy R.E. who also are working on deep dugouts at V.14.b.	
"	9/5/18			
"	10/5/18		Electric round BOUZINCOURT & crossroads	
"	11/5/18		proceeding at night roads passing through the line also blocked by trees including NORTHUMBERLAND AVENUE.	
"	12/5/18			
"	13/5/18		Erecting small steel shelter in bank near x roads in V.12.c. for reserve Bn. centre Brigade	
"	14/5/18			
"	15/5/18		2/Lt J.G. BOWEN 14th R.W.F. joined for duty, as o/c attached infy. JV	

WAR DIARY
or
INTELLIGENCE SUMMARY

(Erase heading not required.)

Army Form C. 2118

123rd FIELD COMPANY
ROYAL ENGINEERS.

Instructions regarding War Diaries and Intelligence Summaries are contained in F. S. Regs., Part II. and the Staff Manual respectively. Title Pages will be prepared in manuscript.

Place	Date	Hour	Summary of Events and Information	Remarks and references to Appendices
V.8.q.7.7.	16/5/18			
"	17/5/18		March to Bluff vacated by Reserve Bn 113 Brigade. Recommence work on 2 tunnel dugouts for 2 platoons in ENGLEBELMER. BOUZINCOURT LINE. Visit from C.R.E. 35th & 38th Div. & on 20.5.18 re taking over.	weather hot & sultry
To V.5.a. Bluff near HEDAUVILLE WOOD	18/5/18		Work as for 17th. visit from 2nd in cd. 205 re shelters etc. this handed over on 20th.	dummy
"	19/5/18	9.45am	Gas shelling during the night in area east & south of camp. Handing over work to officers of 203, 204 & 205 Fd. Coys. meeting with CRE & OC 151st training programme	this period
"		5pm	O.C. to TOUTENCOURT to see CRE re BELL A+B tanks shall about this time near WARROY-VARENNES road	
" to PRISONERS of WAR CAGE TOUTENCOURT	20/5/18	5AM	Coy march to camp of 20 Section at TOUTENCOURT & take over huts & tents in & near PRISONERS of WAR CAGE.	J.Y.

Army Form C. 2118

WAR DIARY
or
INTELLIGENCE SUMMARY

123rd FIELD COMPANY,
ROYAL ENGINEERS.

(Erase heading not required.)

Instructions regarding War Diaries and Intelligence Summaries are contained in F. S. Regs., Part II. and the Staff Manual respectively. Title Pages will be prepared in manuscript.

Place	Date	Hour	Summary of Events and Information	Remarks and references to Appendices
PRISONERS OF WAR CAMP TOUTENCOURT	21		See Training programme. Inspection of Musketry on 30 x 30 yds range. 2/L MORGAN & party 10am + 12 oR. Report to A.P.M. in BELL	weather JW
"	22		Sapper R.BELL shot at dawn.	warm
"	23		hours of training advanced an hour ie 6am, 8am during warm weather, to revert back for marching etc not to take place between 9am + 3pm during hot weather (Clock order)	weather cooler
"	24		attached infantry ordered to rejoin their units forthwith will rejoin Recoys on return of Divn to line.	a lot of wind, some rain
"	25		informal inspection of transport by C.R.E. full programme arranged.	weather warmer
"	26		Sunday church parade C of E 9 am. nonconformist 2 pm. ayres inspection & musketry	JW

Army Form C. 2118

WAR DIARY
or
INTELLIGENCE SUMMARY
(Erase heading not required.)

123rd FIELD COMPANY
ROYAL ENGINEERS.

Instructions regarding War Diaries and Intelligence Summaries are contained in F. S. Regs., Part II. and the Staff Manual respectively. Title Pages will be prepared in manuscript.

Place	Date	Hour	Summary of Events and Information	Remarks and references to Appendices
PRISONERS OF WAR CAMP TOUTENCOURT	27		See revised programme of training. Coy in attack in open.	
"	28	6pm	Rehearsal for instruction by Coys Commander V Corps along with 114 Brigade group.	
"	29		Defence of post in wood. Instruction rifle competition. No 4 section won comp A	
"	30	10.30 am	Inspection by Coys Commander V Corps. Instruction rifle competition. No 3 section won comp B.	fine
"	30	9 am	2nd Coy. R.E. rifle competition. No 4 section beat no 2 section 151 comp A. No 3 section beat no 3 section 157 comp B. HQ 151 beat HQ 123 comp C. Drivers etcs 151 beat 123 " E Mounted NCOs 123 " F	fine warm
"	31	8am 10am 2pm	Outposts in wood. Inspection of Coy by OC	fine warm

J Wood Major RE
OC 123 Fd Coy RE

PROGRAMME OF TRAINING - 123rd Field Co. R.E

1st day ~~Monday~~ Tuesday 21/5/18.
  Morning – Inspection of Kits, stores etc. Cleaning up generally. Anti-Gas Inspection and Dril ½ hour.
  Afternoon – Baths, Firing.

2nd day Wednesday 22nd.
  Morning – Physical Training, Firing, Saluting Squad Drill, Rifle exercises.
  Afternoon – Company attends Matinee given by Divl. Concert Party.
  Evening – Reconnaissance of RED Line by Officers and N.C.O's.

3rd day Thursday 23rd
  Physical Training, Bayonet Fighting Anti-Gas Drill, Rifle Exercises Musketry, Firing.

4th day Friday 24th
  Physical Training, Squad Drill, Anti-Gas Drill, Extended Order Musketry, Firing.

5th day Saturday 25th
  Physical Training, Bayonet Fighting Visual Training. Preliminary Inspection Parade of Company with Transport.
  Firing.
  Road Reconnaissance in connection with Defence Scheme - Off. and N.C.Os

6th day Sunday 26th
  Morning – Church Parades - C.of E. and Non.Com. Anti-Gas Drill, Firing.

7th day Monday 27th
  Scheme of Attack - Company. Musketry and Firing.
  Evening – Brigade Rehearsal for Inspection by Corps Commander.

8th day Tuesday 28th
  Anti-Gas Drill, Scheme for Defence - Company. Firing Competition - Inter-Section.

9th day Wednesday 29th
  Morning – Brigade Inspection by Corps Commander.
  Afternoon – Firing.

10th day Thursday 30th
  Firing Competitions against 151st Field Co. R.E. Inspection of Draught and Riding Horses in connection with Competition

11th day Friday 31st
  Outpost Scheme for Company. Baths, Cleaning up. Full Parade with Transport for O's C. Inspection at 2 p.m.

Secret.

Original
War Diary. June. 1918.

123 Field Coy. R.E.   38 (Welsh) Divn.

30.6.18.

Army Form C. 2118

WAR DIARY
or
INTELLIGENCE SUMMARY
(Erase heading not required.)

Instructions regarding War Diaries and Intelligence Summaries are contained in F.S. Regs., Part II. and the Staff Manual respectively. Title Pages will be prepared in manuscript.

Place	Date	Hour	Summary of Events and Information	Remarks and references to Appendices
FOUNTENCOURT	1/6/18		C.R.E. inspects the Company. In the inter-company Competition for the best Section Prize awarded to No. 1. Section of 123rd Field Coy R.E.	
DO.	2/6/18		Coy. Sports.	
DO.	3/6/18		Company attended Matinée given by the "DUDS"	
DO.	4/6/18		Advance Party left to take over from 247. Field Coy.	
DO.	5/6/18		Three Sections moved into the line and occupied billets in ENGLEBELMER.	
DO.	6/6/18		H.Q. and No. 3. Section moved to CLAIRFAYE FME.	

Army Form C. 2118

WAR DIARY
or
INTELLIGENCE SUMMARY
(Erase heading not required.)

Instructions regarding War Diaries and Intelligence Summaries are contained in F.S. Regs, Part II. and the Staff Manual respectively. Title Pages will be prepared in manuscript.

Place	Date	Hour	Summary of Events and Information	Remarks and references to Appendices
Fosseux	7/6/18.		No 4 Section working with 113th Inf. Bde. Nos. 1 & 2 Section " under C.R.E. No. 3 in Reserve on Tracks	
ENGLEBELMER	8/6/18		Do.	
Do	9/6/18.		Do.	
Do	10/6/18.		Do.	
Do	11/6/18.		Change over of Section. No. 3 Section relieves No. 4 Section. Nos 1 & 2 working under C.R.E. Capt McKean relieves O.C. Coy. Billets at ENGLEBELMER taken over by 14 R.W.F. Coy moves into new billets in "FORCEVILLE".	
FORCEVILLE	12/6/18		Coy. Billeted. Shelled with H.V.s.	[signature]

WAR DIARY or INTELLIGENCE SUMMARY

Army Form C. 2118

Place	Date	Hour	Summary of Events and Information	Remarks and references to Appendices
FOREVILLE	13/6/18		Coy Billets shelled by the enemy - Men's bivouacs moved into a new position	
Do.	14/6/18		Work on the Intermediate System proceeding satisfactorily.	
Do.	15/6/18		Sappers detailed for special operation on the enemy's fenced commenced training with 14 Batt. R.W.F.	
Do.	16/6/18		Visited left sector with C.R.E. and decided on position of C.T. which is to form support line to QUAKER ALLEY.	
Do.	17/6/18		Major Wood on leave. Change over of Nos. 2 & 4 sections	
Do.	18/6/18		2nd Lt Middleton reported for duty.	

Army Form C. 2118

WAR DIARY
or
INTELLIGENCE SUMMARY
(Erase heading not required.)

Instructions regarding War Diaries and Intelligence Summaries are contained in F.S. Regs., Part II. and the Staff Manual respectively. Title Pages will be prepared in manuscript.

Place	Date	Hour	Summary of Events and Information	Remarks and references to Appendices
FORCEVILLE	19/6/18		Called to see Adj. R.E. & fixed up 3 details regarding charges re. for the Raids.	
Do.	20/6/18		All working parties cancelled	
Do.	21/6/18		All working parties cancelled. 14th R.W.F. & 2nd R.W.F. raided evening trenches in front of "HAMEL".	
Do.	22/6/18		Brigade relief. 115 Iny Bde relieved 113 Iny Bde.	
Do.	23/6/18		1st Belt of wire in front of machine intermediate system completed between QUAKER ALLEY and GRASS AV.	
Do.	24/6/18		Nos. 1 & 2 Sections change over.	
Do.	25/6/18		Steeles transport lined.	
Do.	26/6/18		Inspected work on the line with Major Fraser	mwh

Army Form C. 2118

WAR DIARY
or
INTELLIGENCE SUMMARY
(Erase heading not required.)

Instructions regarding War Diaries and Intelligence Summaries are contained in F.S. Regs., Part II. and the Staff Manual respectively. Title Pages will be prepared in manuscript.

Place	Date	Hour	Summary of Events and Information	Remarks and references to Appendices
FOREVILLE	27/6/18.		Horse Boards held in QUAKER ALLEY. Batt. relief.	
DO	28/6/18.		Div. Front taken over as a one Bde. Front by 115 Inf. Bde. 114 Inf. Bde. in support on PURDLE SYSTEM. 113 Inf. Bde. in Reserve. Support Batt. ceased work on Intermediate System under R.E.	
DO	29/6/18.		Visited site of Rifle Ranges for the 113 Inf. Bde and arranged details for work. Driver Charles Speed wounded up the lime & two horses. Speed managed to get the transport back to transport lines altho' he himself was wounded.	
DO	30/6/18.		Visited work in the line with Col. Grant Dalton acting C.R.E. Charge over of No. 1. & 3 Sections.	

Geo. Mc Kean Capt RE

Secret.

Original War Diary.

123 Field Compy. Royal Engineers

38 (Welsh) Division

1-8-18

Army Form C. 2118

WAR DIARY
or
INTELLIGENCE SUMMARY

122nd FIELD COMPANY
ROYAL ENGINEERS.

(Erase heading not required.)

Place	Date	Hour	Summary of Events and Information	Remarks and references to Appendices
FORCEVILLE	1/7/18		No. 1 Section Employed on Intermediate System	
			" 2 " " " Purple System	
			" 3 " " in Reserve.	
			" 4 " " with Front Line Bde.	
Do.	2/7/18		183 Inf Bde relieved 115 Inf Bde.	
Do.	3/7/18		Col. Frankfoult a/CRE. called ref. work on Intermediate System and handing over Same to 124 Field Cy R.E. 123 Field Company to be responsible for all work on Purple System.	
Do.	4/7/18		Work on Purple System proceeding satisfactorily.	
Do.	5/7/18		Met C.R.E. Chief Engineer & G.S.O.I. ref work on Concrete Cupolas — Sites for these were selected.	
Do.	6/7/18		Bn. Relief returned. Major Wood returned.	

Army Form C. 2118

WAR DIARY
or
INTELLIGENCE SUMMARY

123rd FIELD COMPANY
ROYAL ENGINEERS.

(Erase heading not required.)

Instructions regarding War Diaries and Intelligence Summaries are contained in F.S. Regs., Part II. and the Staff Manual respectively. Title Pages will be prepared in manuscript.

Place	Date	Hour	Summary of Events and Information	Remarks and references to Appendices
FORCEVILLE				
Do	7/7/18		Called in to see G.O.C. 114 Inf Bde re work. Visits site of M.G. Emplts with C.R.S.	
Do	8/7/18		Sites exact position of Emplts.	
Do	9/7/18		Bde Relief. 115 Inf Bde relieves 113 Inf Bde.	
Do	10/7/18		With C.R.E. & Adjt. arranging for materials & for Emplts. Fines peepholes with M.G. Officer. Arranged details for work with 114 Inf Bde.	
Do	11/7/18		M.G. Emplts at P.14.a.20.45 commenced. 26 Inf Bde bringing up material for Emplts.	
Do	12/7/18		Called at C.R.E's re R.E. stores. Visits Cay. Marshall re Emplts.	
Do	13/7/18		Handed over work for Purple system to Lt Morgan. Lt Lethom M.G. Emplts.	MWh

1875 Wt. W 593/826 1,000,000 4/15 J.R.C. & A. A.D.S.S./Forms/C. 2118.

Army Form C. 2118

WAR DIARY
or
INTELLIGENCE SUMMARY

(Erase heading not required.)

123rd FIELD COMPANY
ROYAL ENGINEERS.

Instructions regarding War Diaries and Intelligence Summaries are contained in F.S. Regs., Part II. and the Staff Manual respectively. Title Pages will be prepared in manuscript.

Place	Date	Hour	Summary of Events and Information	Remarks and references to Appendices
FORCEVILLE	14/7/18		Arranged details for work on M.G. Emplt. at Q19.b.9.8. Camouflage taken up.	
Do.	15/7/18		Handing over work to O.C. 97 Field Coy. Purple system and M.G. Emplt.	
Do.	16/7/18		Handing over Front line's work to O.C. 97. F.C.R.S.	
Do.	17/7/18		Relief of Div. Cancelled. Battle Supplies returned to Transport lines.	
Do.	18/7/18		Handing over work to O.C. 247 Field Coy, and 240 Field Coy.	
Do.	19/7/18		Coy. moves to Toutencourt - relieves by 247 Field Coy. R.E.	
Toutencourt	20/7/18		Cleaning Camp, cleaning wagons, whole day. Cut-employed.	

Army Form C. 2118

WAR DIARY
or
INTELLIGENCE SUMMARY
(Erase heading not required.)

123rd FIELD COMPANY
ROYAL ENGINEERS.

Place	Date	Hour	Summary of Events and Information	Remarks and references to Appendices
TOUTENCOURT.	21/7/18		Sections on Musketry & Drill.	
Do.	22/7/18		2 Sections on Musketry Drill & Demolitions.	
Do.	23/7/18		2 Sections on Musketry &c. 2 Section on Range for 113 & 114 Inf Bde.	
Do.	24/7/18		No. 4 Section ceased work on Ranges.	
Do.	25/7/18		Sections on Musketry & Lewis Gunnery - Instruction detailed to assist form 113 Inf Bde.	
Do.	26/7/18		Coy. Employed Preparing Rounds for Divi. Horseshow.	
Do.	27/7/18		Ditto. & Lewis Gunnery.	
Do.	28/7/18		Inter Coy. Sports.	
Do	29/7/18		Inter Section Competition in Shooting - Prize taken by No. 2 Section	

Army Form C. 2118

WAR DIARY
or
INTELLIGENCE SUMMARY
(Erase heading not required.)

123rd FIELD COMPANY
ROYAL ENGINEERS.

Place	Date	Hour	Summary of Events and Information	Remarks and references to Appendices
TOUTENCOURT.	30/7/18		All sections on musketry. Drill & harness cleaning. Competition for best Pair of draught Horses & harness won by Dr. Collins.	
Do.	31/7/18		Coy. relieved 158th Field Coy. working on M.S. Ginger & Avon system. No. 3 & 4 sections working on left. " 1 & 2 " " " Right. Transport lines remained at Toutencourt.	

Scrutchean Capt RE
O.C. 123rd Fld. Coy.

SECRET

Vol 33

ORIGINAL WAR DIARY

AUGUST 1918

123 FIELD COY R.E.

38th DIVISION

Army Form C. 2118

WAR DIARY
or
INTELLIGENCE SUMMARY
(Erase heading not required.)

123 Field Coy. R.E.

Place	Date	Hour	Summary of Events and Information	Remarks and references to Appendices
FORCEVILLE	1/8/18		Work commenced on concrete Pill Boxes.	
Ditto	2/8/18		Nos. 1 & 2 moved to join Nos. 3 & 4 Sections in Sappers Valley V. & C. 8.8.	
SAPPERS VALLEY nr HEMANVILLE	3/8/18		Gas Shorts - 1 Casualty from the Coy.	
Ditto	4/8/18		Our Stone Show - 1 Casualty from the Coy. Orders received to relieve 78 Field Coy. on this Relig.	
Ditto	5/8/18		Our Relief -	
Ditto	6/8/18		Ditto	
Ditto	7/8/18		Ditto. Two 1 Pillbox at W.7.2.3.4. commenced. Battle Supplies 1 W.C.O. & 3 men per Section formed.	
Ditto	8/8/18		Major Wood returns back to the Coy. Capt. Milkern visits M.S. Suply. with E.R.E.	

Army Form C. 2118

WAR DIARY
or
INTELLIGENCE SUMMARY
(Erase heading not required.)

Instructions regarding War Diaries and Intelligence Summaries are contained in F.S. Regs., Part II. and the Staff Manual respectively. Title Pages will be prepared in manuscript.

Place	Date	Hour	Summary of Events and Information	Remarks and references to Appendices
SAPPERS VALLEY nr HEADAUVILLE	9/8/18		Made arrangements with 20S. U.S. Engineers Regt. for 1 platoon to work on M.S. Enys 8. Prepared mine at V.3.b.80.15.	
Ditto	10/8/18.		No.108/05 Cpl. M.F. Davis wounded near Hedauville & sub-sequently died of wounds at the CCS.	
Ditto	11/8/18.		Nos. 1 & 4 Platoons 7. Eng. 30th U.S. Engineers Regt. to work on mine M.S. Enys.	
Ditto	12/8/18.		Major Wood at Hqrs. of CRE. Col. Kerball CRE 38. Div. & CE. 1st Corps.	
Ditto	13/8/18.		Lt Doyle went on leave to England	
Ditto	14/8/18.		Transport lines moved from TOUTENCOURT to V.11.a.4.0. Lt. Michelin reconnoitered Bridges & approaches at Q.35 central Railway Bridge to be reconstructed. 2 culverts to be formed & one Bridge on East side of ANCRE.	
Ditto	15/8/18.		Main Pill Box at V.6.a.2.3. completed	
Ditto	16/8/18.		Materials for bridging & taken up to MESNIL.	J.W.

1875 Wt. W593/826 1,000,000 4/15 J.B.C. & A. A.D.S.S./Forms/C. 2118.

Army Form C. 2118

WAR DIARY
or
INTELLIGENCE SUMMARY
(Erase heading not required.)

Instructions regarding War Diaries and Intelligence Summaries are contained in F. S. Regs., Part II. and the Staff Manual respectively. Title Pages will be prepared in manuscript.

Place	Date	Hour	Summary of Events and Information	Remarks and references to Appendices
SAPPERS VALLEY NR. HERDAUVILLE	17/8/18		Capt W.Adams C.B. 159th Field Coy. to relieve Capt Millar who proceded on leave to England	
"	18/8/18	11am	lecture on camouflage by V Corps camouflage officer	
"	19/8/18	11am	Major Wood attending Conference at Corps Div HQ as C.R.E. 38th Div. "Secrecy essential"	
"	20-8-18	9 pm	C.R.E. held conference at 123 Coy H.Q. re follow up arrangements in case of Enemy withdrawal from THIEPVAL - OVILLERS area. Concrete work kept up.	
"	21-8-18		Major Wood took over Coy from Capt Evans. Col. KENSON having returned to D.H.Q. from C.E.'s office on 20.8.18.	
"		9.45am	Div pontoons & 6 pontoons & 3 trestles given No 3 Pontoon Pk. taken to MARTINSART Wood	
"	22/8/18	11 pm	Sections orded up to Bn HQrs 114 Brigade to assist in crossing ANCRE by means of footbridges. If the CHICKWEED system was held by Sectn tramway crossing. Nos 2 & 3 Sections HAMEL MILL Bridge. No. 4 Section AUTHUILLE	

WAR DIARY
or
INTELLIGENCE SUMMARY

Army Form C. 2118

Place	Date	Hour	Summary of Events and Information	Remarks and references to Appendices
114 Bn HQ. ENGLEBELMER	22/23		Lt MIDDLETON with No 1 Section reported to Bn. H.Q. Through Brigade H.Q. on arrival. Stores were taken as far as possible without giving away the intention of bridging to the enemy. They fire on this evening	
South CAUSEWAY	1918		Lt MORGAN with No 4 Section reported to Bn. H.Q. + through Brigade to O.C. He was informed that No infantry had gone over this crossing + none were going over that night. Enemy M.G. fire on this crossing.	
AUTHUILE crossing				
HAMEL MILL			Lt GRIFFITHS with Nos 2+3 Sections could not get Transport to HAMEL as this road had not yet been cleared by the Pioneers. He took bridging material for HAMEL MILL to QUAKER ALLEY and went to find Major HELM. 9/G.O. 15th Wel. who was reported by 114 Brigade to be at Bn. H.Q. of Div on left opposite St. PIERRE D'IVION. Lt. GRIFFITHS went there but could not find O.C. 15th Wel though he met Br. Gen. GWYN-THOMAS commanding Right Brigade of Div on our left. Work done stores taken as far as possible & camouflaged.	J.V.

Place	Date	Hour	Summary of Events and Information	Remarks and references to Appendices
North CAUSEWAY	23-4-1918	8.45 pm	No movement was to be visible to enemy before this hour	
		9.15	Infantry were to start crossing & work to begin by R.E. Brigr also wished another bridge at HAMEL footbridge rather than South Causeway. HAMEL MILL Bridge taken over by 17th Div R.E. AUTHUILLE Bridge was not required by 114 Brigade. 50 Pnrs. were available for carrying cork rafts. Nos 1+4 Sections were detailed for No III crossing i.e. "North Causeway" Nos 2+3 " " " " HAMEL Bridge. On arrival at foot of HESNIL AUTHUILLE hill it was found impossible to get horse transport along the road to HAMEL as this had not yet been made good by the Pioneers who were working on the HESNIL-HAMEL Road as ordered. Cork rafts (about a 4 man load by day) had to be carried in the dark some 400 x over barbed wire entanglements, shell holes, broken railway lines etc. When 114 were in Nos 2+3 were found to be more than 300' of swamp. Seeing the difficulty No 1+4 were put to assist + the Brigadier 114 was informed personally by O.C. 123 Coy. JW	

Army Form C. 2118

WAR DIARY
or
INTELLIGENCE SUMMARY
(Erase heading not required.)

Instructions regarding War Diaries and Intelligence Summaries are contained in F. S. Regs., Part II. and the Staff Manual respectively. Title Pages will be prepared in manuscript.

Place	Date	Hour	Summary of Events and Information	Remarks and references to Appendices
NORTH CAUSEWAY ANCRE VALLEY	23 24 1918	9.15	Owing to the Brigadiers arrangements that the infantry were to start crossing as soon as or rather before the bridge work could be started in making the bridge there was naturally much congestion in carrying up cork rafts (a 6 man load by night) along a track & bridge for infantry in single file. The infantry men however got over somehow though in places the water was 7 feet deep.	enemy retaliation light some H.E. near Bn H.Q. MESNIL
		12 m	The bridge completed for Lewis gunners to cross. The machine gunners the latter crossing the bridge about 1 am.	+ M.G.fire at MESNIL HAMEL Rd
		1 am	The O.C. again reported to Bde H.Q. after seeing there were I understand no casualties at this crossing on this night the enemy being ignorant of the spot we had selected. He was putting M.G.F. shell fire on the crossing both above & below this one. Thinking North Causeway too bad for any crossing in force. The Officers & men at the bridge head were working waist deep in water	also H.E. at Railway embankment at West end of crossing

1875 Wt. W593/826 1,000,000 4/15 J.B.C. & A. A.D.S.S./Forms/C. 2118.

WAR DIARY
or
INTELLIGENCE SUMMARY

Army Form C. 2118

Instructions regarding War Diaries and Intelligence Summaries are contained in F.S. Regs., Part II. and the Staff Manual respectively. Title Pages will be prepared in manuscript.

(Erase heading not required.)

Place	Date	Hour	Summary of Events and Information	Remarks and references to Appendices
SAPPER VALLEY to "City" shelters East	24	5.30pm	Sapper Section move up to new billets East of ENGLEBELMER. Forced (Engelbeart) on MARTINSART Road. Transport lines move to N. of SENLIS. Start work on AUTHUILLE crossing. Roving in 4° & Field Guns	
ENGLEBELMER		7.30pm	Reconnoitre crossing with C.R.E. & decide route. N.B. Pioneers had started work on approach road to this at 3 p.m. (see tracing of plan & sections of crossing)	
AUTHUILLE crossing	25th	5pm	Bridge tracing complete for field guns & infantry. C.E. visited bridge & gave instructions to make good for 60 pr. by putting in extra roadbearers under wheels	
		7pm	Bridge complete for 60prs (Culvert did not arrive until bridge was complete so 8'6" was used near horse lines	
"	26th 27th		Transport moved to Pioneer Road improving approaches, traffic #A & Sections "	

WAR DIARY
or
INTELLIGENCE SUMMARY

(Erase heading not required.)

Army Form C. 2118

Place	Date	Hour	Summary of Events and Information	Remarks and references to Appendices
AUTHUILLE crossing	28th		inspecting approaches, taking readings of units about below bridge.	
"	29th		Lt. DOYLE rejoins from leave. work on approaches to railway crossing ↑ up to AVELUY-THIEPVAL road	
POZIERES Road	30th	7am	O.C. & Lt. MIDDLETON visit H.Q. Pros. near ¼ 24 Sct. 67. A4. m. also 114 B. Transport Lines BAZENTIN LE PETIT Wood. at CONTALMAISON.	
PIONEER Road	31st	6.30 am	Lt. GRIFFITHS on leave to England. Coy. move up to LONGEVAL for work on road to GINCHY	31.11.15. cool with slight mist rain
"			Horse lines to CONTALMAISON.	

J.C.T. Ward Major R.E.
O.C. 123 Field Coy R.E.

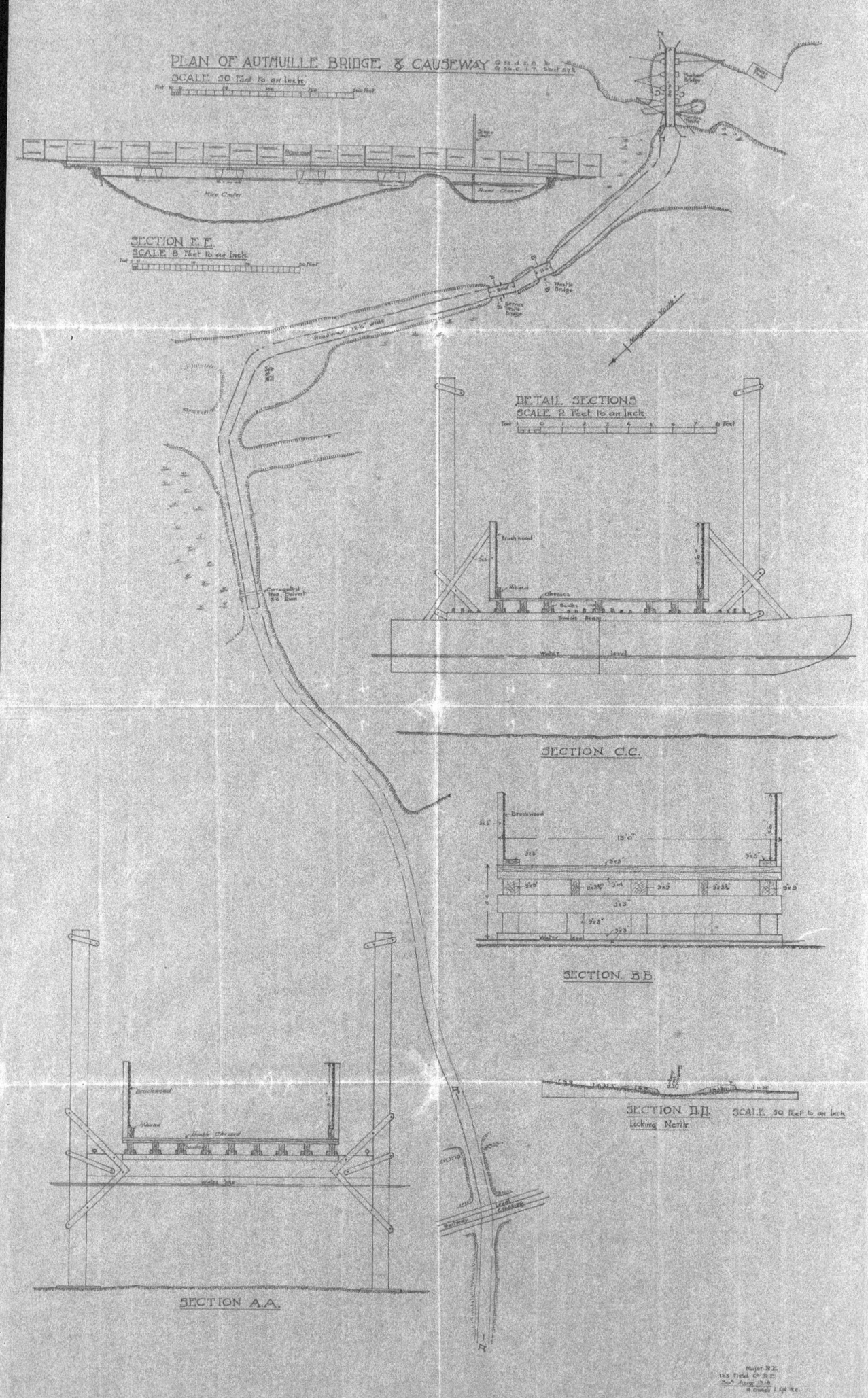

Army Form C. 2118.

WAR DIARY
or
INTELLIGENCE SUMMARY.
(Erase heading not required.)

Vol 34

WAR DIARY

123rd Fld Coy R E

1st September 1918 to 30th September 1918.

N.A.T. Priestley
Major R.E.

Army Form C. 2118

WAR DIARY
INTELLIGENCE SUMMARY
(Erase heading not required.)

123rd Field Coy. R.E.

Place	Date	Hour	Summary of Events and Information	Remarks and references to Appendices
LONGEVAL	1/9/16		Work on roads LONGEVAL – GINCHY (slab road) GINCHY-LESBOEUFS Horse lines to BAZENTIN repairs	
"	2nd		"	
"	3rd	1pm	ditto to 7pm	
		1pm	Received orders to start on Adv. Gd. 3d. Coy. under B.G. 114 Brigade with pontoons to bridge TORTILLE. Coy to report to "North Copse" to SAILLY-SAILLISEL. O.C. to Brig at SAILLY church. Coy moves to Brig. O.C. to report road good to govt farm. Cyclists patrol forward roads & report road good to govt farm. Made good road	
SAILLY-SAILLISEL		5pm	Coy at SAILLY. Nos 2 Section proceeds to Govt Fm to MANAN COURT for pontoons which percied at dusk up far as far as possible sunken road remaining sections push up approaches & crossings of sunken road E of SAILLY	
			Lt. DOYLE & MORGAN reconnoitre Nos 2 & 4 Sections at Br. H.Q.	
SAILLY	17th	6 am	Nos 1 & 3 with pontoons Home time return to GINCHY for motoring facilities	
		12 noon		
			Nos 2 & 4 now move up to Br. H.Q. & rec. for advance. Nos 2 & 4 now move up to Br. H.A. & rec. for bridges 14th Bn held H.Q. shelled adjt 4RSM wounded + a labour et...	
		5pm		
		6.30pm	report re crossings to Brigade H.Q. G.801 then gives orders for pontoon Br.	

WAR DIARY
or
INTELLIGENCE SUMMARY

(Erase heading not required.)

Army Form C. 2118

Instructions regarding War Diaries and Intelligence Summaries are contained in F.S. Regs., Part II. and the Staff Manual respectively. Title Pages will be prepared in manuscript.

Place	Date	Hour	Summary of Events and Information	Remarks and references to Appendices
SAILLY ETRICOURT MANANCOURT	4	Night 4/5	Pontoon teams sent up to MANANCOURT hooked in & took trestle pontoons to site. Area & central Lts. DOYLE & MORGAN constructing light bridge. Lt. MIDDLETON repairing road bridge at MANANCOURT good for 6 tons.	Solution of bridge at Manancourt
"	5	10am	report at Bn HQ from Lt. DOYLE new pontoon required to width of CANAL DU NORD being greater than shewn in Sectional plans. C.R.E. for new pontoon & details of Heavy bridge for C.E. & Corps as received from Lt. DOYLE. 124 ton pontoon also pontoon from Point drawn by M.T. #151 Coy. 11th Pontoon sent up to assist. gave the shelling of cutting and Bn HQ	at Manancourt and upper (& forms attached) Appendix A.
ETRICOURT		Night 5/6	Lt. MORGAN with no 4 Section & men from 151 Complete light Canadian pontoon bridge opposite ETRICOURT	
MANANCOURT		5/6	Lt. MIDDLETON +1 +3 gcv. Completing repairs to MANANCOURT Bridge & repairing CRIB PIER Bridge South of it. Both good for heavy traffic	
SAILLY			Lt. DOYLE repairing trestle bridge in SAILLY for heavy traffic. Can take 13 ton tractor & 9.2's	
SAILLY	6		shelled in SAILLY to prevent sagging of roadbearers. Casualties 30 mostly gassed by mixed relieved by Coys of 21st Div H.E. & gas shelling of MANANCOURT Coy. returned to LONGUEVAL 6 subsequently left in	

WAR DIARY
or
INTELLIGENCE SUMMARY

Army Form C. 2118

Place	Date	Hour	Summary of Events and Information	Remarks and references to Appendices
LONGUEVAL	7		Sections setting & battn. 124 & 151 alongside in S.10.c.	
"	8		Reconnaissance of huts in area for Corps north from Div 3rd officers	
To BEAUVENCOURT	9	9am	3 Corps move to BEAUVENCOURT & camp at Div. Rec. camp on VILLERS AU FLOS Road	
		2pm	Commence work on lookhouses, huts etc. for Div. Rec. camp.	
"	10		" Commence work on YPRES ETRICOURT road & on fillings	17th div.
"	11		O's visit site for camp on YPRES ETRICOURT road & on Div camp ETRICOURT with view to taking over on 11th. Move postponed to 12th but 124 & 151 work up to new camp.	
East of LE MESNIL	12		log. Move to YPRES-ETRICOURT road in V.2 a+b 124 & 151 alongside. Commence work on approaches to waterpoints. Battn complete must 3am after section left at Div? Rec. camp to continue work on camp.	H.V.Shelling & bombing by night
"	13		work on approaches to waterpoints & roads	"
"	14		Major Dickinson visits Div HQ re work there	"
"	15		Visit battery & drying room on EVRICOURT EQUANCOURT road. Nos 1 & 2 sections to work with Br 124 on Br HQs drying room near FINS - GOUZEAUCOURT road. No 3 section at Div HQ camp. No 4 section Battn drying room.	"
"	16		Transport of 3 pontoon wagons to CRE HQ for moving frames & trips to 16th.	15th

1875 W. W593/826 1,000,000 4/15 J.B.C. & A. A.D.S.S./Forms/C. 2118.

WAR DIARY
or
INTELLIGENCE SUMMARY

(Erase heading not required.)

Army Form C. 2118

Place	Date	Hour	Summary of Events and Information	Remarks and references to Appendices
LECHELLE	17	4 am	ordered to mark out Track with avenues on Drying ground & Div HQ. Track for H.T. from Camel Track to E. of FINS to be completed by 9am. reported completion 8.30 am. Major J.C.I. Wood ordered to report to Director of Works. Handing over log to 2/Lt DOYLE.	J MacGregor C.R.E. 1.23 February 18. 17/9/1918
LECHELLE	17 18	5 PM 8 AM	Major J.C.I. Wood left to report to Director of Works. Two sections Nos 3 & 4 under OC of No 1 Coy proceed to W.3.a.1.0 & report to C.R.A. for work on forward roads. FINS - GOUZEAUCOURT also HEUDECOURT - NEVELON - GOUZEAUCOURT RDS. made good for all traffic to a point 100 x in front of our line. The division having attacked at 5.20 AM. No 1 & 2 sections working in Div H.Q., Bath Houses, Water Point (Approach) Lieut Dickins on went in leave. Capt. H.A.S. PRESSEY M.C. R.E. took over command of the company	C.S.

Army Form C. 2118

WAR DIARY
or
INTELLIGENCE SUMMARY

(Erase heading not required.)

Instructions regarding War Diaries and Intelligence Summaries are contained in F. S. Regs., Part II. and the Staff Manual respectively. Title Pages will be prepared in manuscript.

Place	Date	Hour	Summary of Events and Information	Remarks and references to Appendices
LECHELLE	19.		No 5 1 and 3 Sections making road at water point 57 C S.E. P 32. d. 7.7.	S.
	20	8am	No 2 and 4 Sections preparing new divisional Hq at 57 C S.W. O 36. c.	S
		1 p.m.	do	S
		2.6/pm	Whole company in divl. Hq at 57C S.W. O 36. c. + party 7 & 19th Bn. Welsh Regt (Pioneers)	
	21.		Whole company in divl. Hq with 120 men 19th Bn. Welsh Regt (Pioneers)	
	22		Whole company in Div. Hq work.	
	23.		Company rested. Rifle + gas mask inspection and Baths	
	24.		Company trenches company drill ammunition	
	25		Company trenches open air work.	
	26		do	
	27		do	
HEUDICOURT	28		Company moved Hq + 4 Sections to HEUDICOURT Sheet 57 C S.E. W 20. a.	S.

Above line at LE SOREL-LE-GRAND W 13. c.

WAR DIARY
INTELLIGENCE SUMMARY
(Erase heading not required.)

Place	Date	Hour	Summary of Events and Information	Remarks and references to Appendices
HEUDICOURT	29		Company started by rail from RIUX [illegible]	
	30		Others arrived at 9 p.m. to get in touch with prisoners who knew we were able to support back. Prisoners were [illegible] equipment and provided by [illegible]. little use. [illegible] [illegible] took from 10.15 hrs till [illegible] [illegible] [illegible] before sent from positions in the neighbourhood of POPLAR TRENCH to the EPÉE PEZIÈRES. Bombs were put further E to prevent the [illegible] to [illegible]. Finally to MALASSISE FARM in W.28.c. Sheet 57A.SE, and 1 am awaiting [illegible] [illegible] arrived from up with a batch. They were [illegible] [illegible] to the [illegible] [illegible] 5/6. Coats [illegible] are occupied the track [illegible] [illegible] [illegible] [illegible] [illegible] from to [illegible] from PARACE SAP to southern [illegible] 57 mm — 2 officers + 2 ranks of 6 Nova Scotia Forward Company had already made 2 ord outs to posts in both trenches W.14.a.5,8 and trenches at X.28.B.5,7 and continued back over GATELET VALLEY to X.28.C.67. Dead bodies lay 9 deep all in [illegible] [illegible] [illegible] [illegible] [illegible] in lieu.	

2/Lt. [illegible]

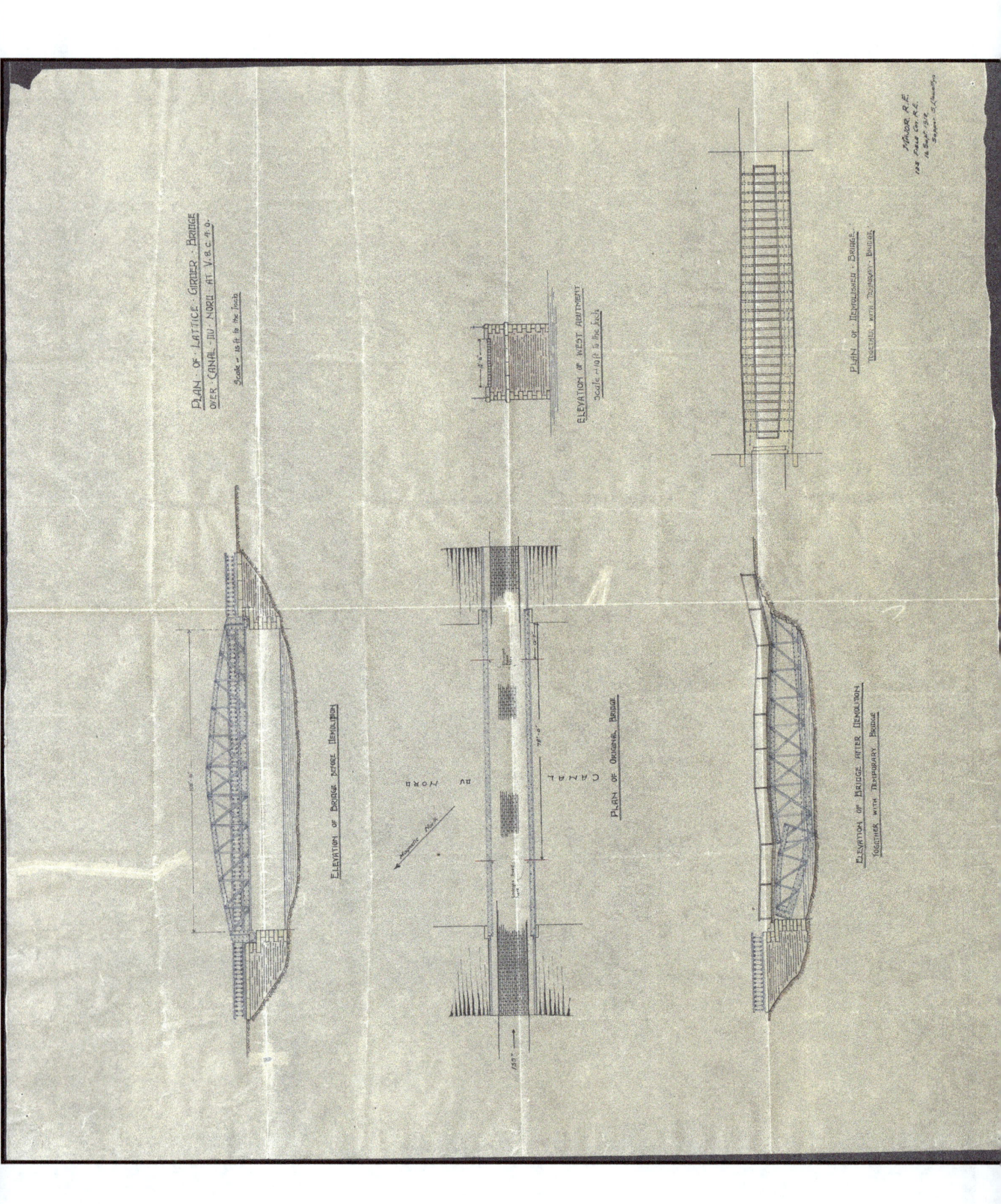

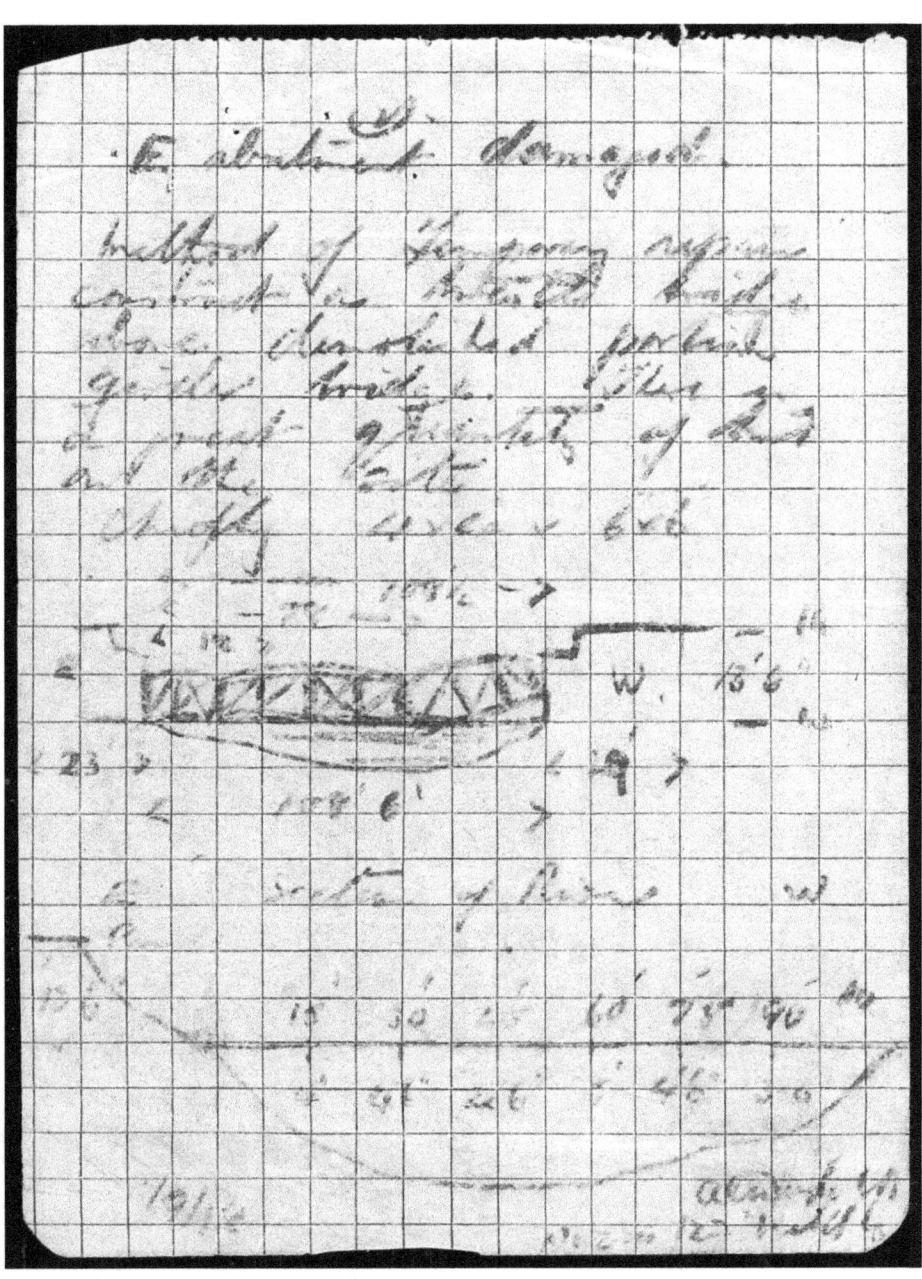

O/C. 123 Field Coy R.E.

I beg to report that I made a reconnaissance of Road Bridge at [redacted] V.8 C 4.0.

The bridge is a steel lattice girder bridge. It is destroyed at a point 76' from W end of girder & has sagged to a point 12' from E end of girder.

Total Span of Girder 108½'
Total Width of Roadway 15'½"
Width of Pier 8'10"
Ht of Road level above water 13'6"
Section of River given in separate sketch
Approaches good each side
Height of Abutment 2'
" " " 2'

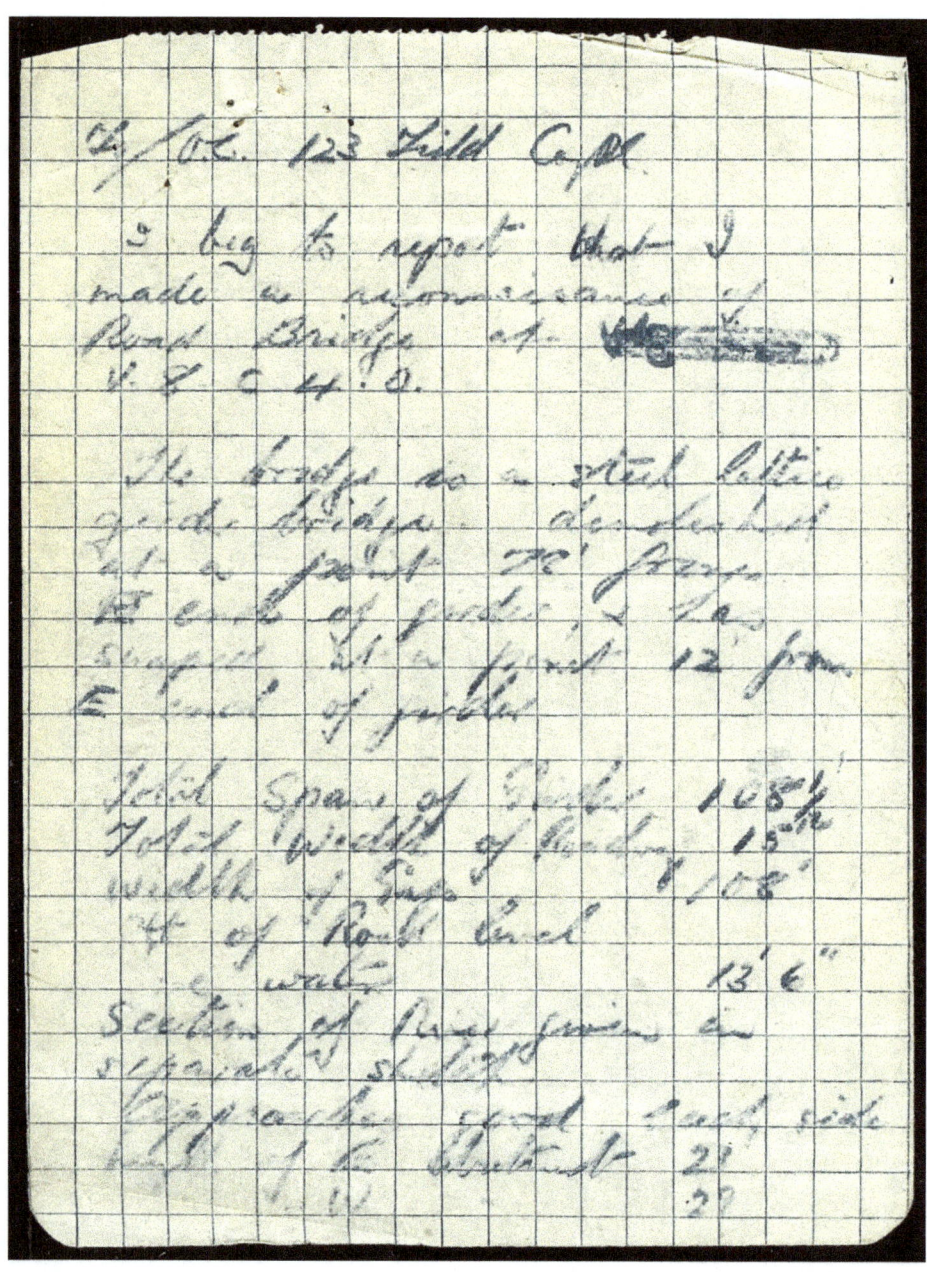

SECTION THROUGH A.B.
Scale - 10 Feet to the Inch

MAJOR R.E.
O.C. 123 Field Company R.E.
25 Sept. 1918
Signed Edmondson

CANAL DU NORD
PLAN OF BRIDGE AT V.8.b.35.30.
Scale - 15 Feet to the Inch

188'·0"

ELEVATION OF BRIDGE

Light Railway

PLAN OF BRIDGE

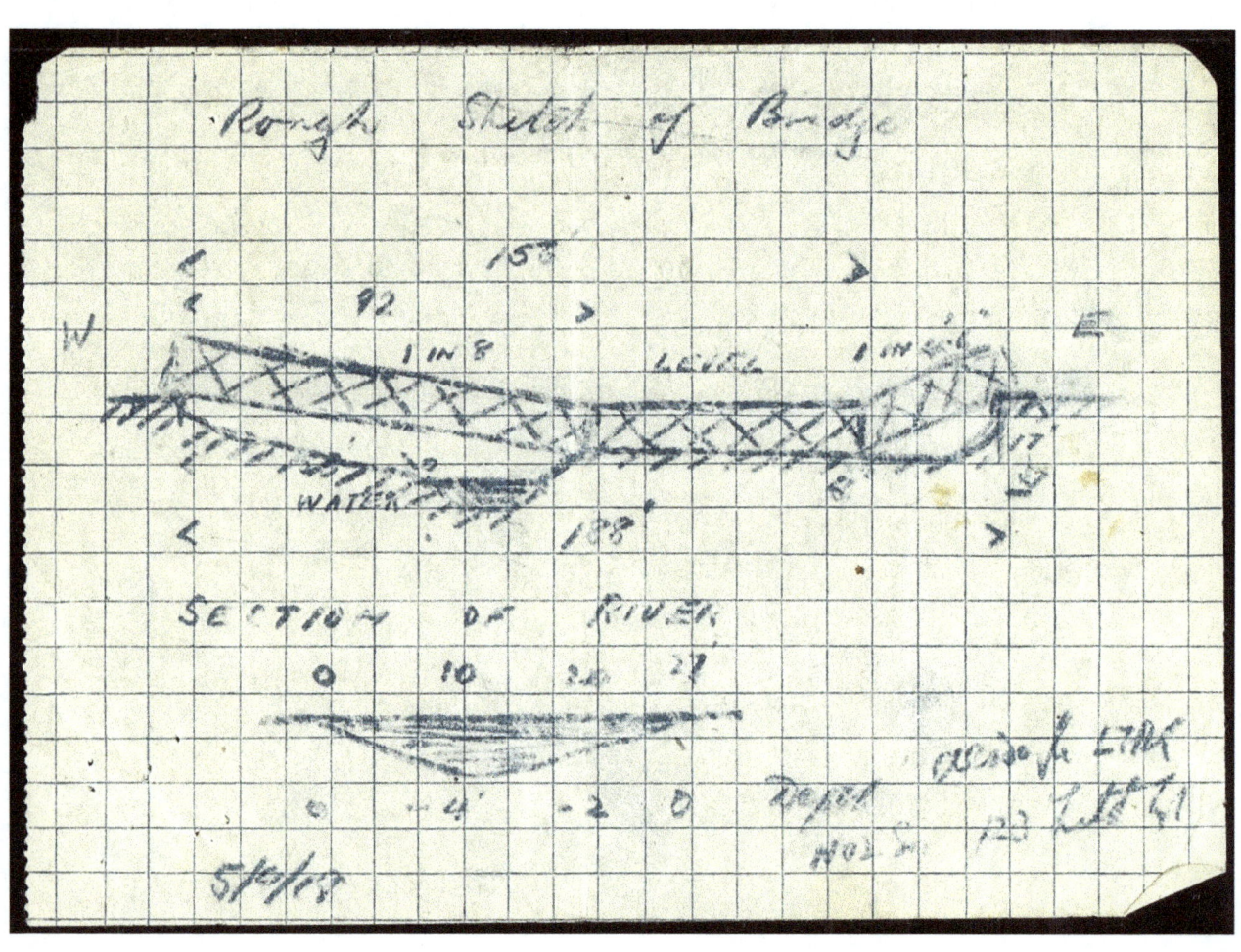

To. O.C.
123 Field Coy R.E.

I beg to report that I made a reconnaissance of Road bridge at. V.8.b.35.50.

The bridge consisted of two RSJ girders. The bridge had been demolished by cutting girder in two places (as p sketch)

Length of girder 185'
Width of Roadway 12'
Total width of CANAL 80'
   at this point
Height of Roadway above
   water level 14'6"
Maximum depth of
   water 4'

Since the demolition of this bridge the girder has remained resting on one (W) abutment & is also resting on opposite bank

(2)

The 3 slopes of roadway
west to east is as follows
92' approx slope 1 in 8
64' " " LEVEL
32' " " 1 in 4.6
This road could be made
suitable for heavy guns etc
if it is timbered over where
required. There is a fair
amount of timber on the spot
for this work.

The approaches on both sides
of bridge are good.

The abutments of the old bridge
are about 15' to the N of others
Approx distance between old
abutments 106'
Abutments 20' long
damaged 30' ¼ destroyed

<u>Secret</u>

Original War Diary

October 1918.

123rd Field Company R.E.
38th (Welsh) Division

Army Form C. 2118.

Nov 35

WAR DIARY
or
INTELLIGENCE SUMMARY.

123rd FIELD COMPANY
ROYAL ENGINEERS.

(Erase heading not required.)

Instructions regarding War Diaries and Intelligence Summaries are contained in F.S. Regs., Part II. and the Staff Manual respectively. Title pages will be prepared in manuscript.

Place	Date	Hour	Summary of Events and Information	Remarks and references to Appendices
IN THE FIELD.	1918 OCTR. 1		10 O.R. on making good/track from SOREL-le-GRAND to GATELET VALLEY. Notice boarding crossings etc. Remainder of Coy. stood by.	
	2		Battle Surplus 12 O.R. reported at Horse Lines. Third Army Orders - Sec. Lieut. G.S.Morgan M.M., awarded Military Cross A/CSM T.H.Rogers M.M., awarded D.C.M.	
	3		Whole Coy. on preparing Divn. Reception Camp W 13b. (Sh.57c.)	
	4		Coy. preparing Divn. Reception Camp at SOREL-le-GRAND and baths in W 13b. (Sh.57c.) Divl. Baths started in the morning completed in the evening. Coy. preparing Divn. Reception Camp at SOREL-le-GRAND and targets for range for SOREL-le-GRAND.	
	5		Coy. marched forward to W 23b. (Sh.68c.) and waited in readiness to advance with 113th Inf. Bde., coming under orders of G.O.C.113 Bde. At 11.30 hrs. it moved forward with advance Guard of 113th Inf. Bde., it being reported the enemy were retiring. The work of the Coy. being to prepare a track from the neighbourhood of A 14b.5.0 via A 9b.across Escaut River to the neighbourhood of Basket wood and Northo Woodyas the situation permitted. The Coy. marched forward in advance of the Brigade and discovered a route which existed fit for horse transport as far as A 9b.7.2. At this point a bridge of 15 ft. span was put across a very broad and deep Communi. Trench of the Hindenberg System. Track reconnoitred up through A 4c.9.3 where a damage bridge across the River Escaut was repaired. the Coy. advancing behind the support waves of the 113th Bde. who were advancing after the retreating Germans. A track was made about A 4c.4.8 through A 4a. (all above map ref. Sh.62b.N.W 1/20.000) to 5.28c. and 8 and 28d. and 5,(Sh.57b.S.T. 1/20.000) to western corner of Basket Wood, this being reached about 18.30 hours. Here the Coy. halted and went into bivouacs in S 16c.4.7. No.3 Section was sent on with the vanguard to help in preparing routes as required. Marching along north edge of wood through 16b. and 17a. they prepared a track to road running through 11a. and c. (above Map Ref.Sh.57b.S.W) Advancing eastward from this place the advance Guard came under heavy	✓ ✓ ✓ ✓

Army Form C. 2118.

WAR DIARY
or
INTELLIGENCE SUMMARY.

123rd FIELD COMPANY
ROYAL ENGINEERS.

(Erase heading not required.)

Instructions regarding War Diaries and Intelligence Summaries are contained in F.S. Regs., Part II. and the Staff Manual respectively. Title pages will be prepared in manuscript.

Place	Date 1918	Hour	Summary of Events and Information	Remarks and references to Appendices
IN THE FIELD	Octr. 5		shell and M.G.fire in the Le Catelet-Nauroy Line Trench in S 12c. Here the O.C. Advance Guard ordered the Sections, after having made good the track to the road in 11a. and c., to return to the Coy. its services being not further required. The Coy. remained in Billets in S 16c. In the evening the Coy. having been allotted positions in the event of counter attack in S 22 to act as a right refused flank to the Brigade, the position was reconnoitred and dispositions made out in case of necessity. B Echelon move to Bosquet Farm near HONNECOURT. No. 2 Section was taken away by C.R.E. for water supply duties to work directly under him, during the following operations being lost to the Company.	
	6		Lieut. W.Dickinson returned from leave Coy. moved forward to positions of assembly west of Mottho Wood, the 113th Brigade being due to attack at 1 a.m. The Coy. was ordered to make, in the event of the attack being successful, strong points in Angelus Orchard neighbourhood of T 3b.1.4 and in T 3b.0.6, the sections to follow behind the rear wave of the Support Battalion, the Brigade advancing as follows:- 13th R.W.F. on the right, 16th R.W.F. on the left, 14th R.W.F. in support The Coy. rendezvous as follows No. 1 Section - 1 Officer and 16 men in the sunk road at S 19b.0.0, Nos. 3 and 4 Sections at S 6d.2.4. The Coy. was in position by 1 hour carrying picks, shovels, and a few cutting tools, wire and pickets. As No. 3 Section had some distance to carry their stores wire and pickets for them were carried on pack animals. Zero was	
	7		at 1.30 hours. At first the Support Battalion did not move forward, reporting it was held up by severe shelling and M.G. fire. At about 5 hr report was received from Brigade that Angelus Orchard had been captured by the 15th R.W.F. and the R.E's were to move forward to consolidate the main body of the 16th R.W.F. who had been held up by uncut wire. Lieut. Dickinson was wounded in the foot just previous to moving forward, but remained at duty until work completed. No. 1 Section on arrival at Angelus Orchard found in position there a body of 6 men of the 15th R.W.F. who stated they had arrived there earlier in the night, had lost touch with everyone, and considered themselves cut off. Lieut. Dickinson	
	8			

Army Form C. 2118.

WAR DIARY
or
INTELLIGENCE SUMMARY.
(Erase heading not required.)

123rd FIELD COMPANY
ROYAL ENGINEERS.

Instructions regarding War Diaries and Intelligence Summaries are contained in F.S. Regs., Part II. and the Staff Manual respectively. Title pages will be prepared in manuscript.

Place	Date	Hour	Summary of Events and Information	Remarks and references to Appendices
IN THE FIELD.	1918 Oct.r. 8		promptly proceeded to make two small Support Points at T 8a.30.45 and 8a.47.52. Several of the enemy surrendered to the Section. These were handed over to the 13th R.W.F. The strong Points were reported finished at 11.00 hours and were garrisoned by the Infantry of the 14th R.W.F., the Section returning to Billets. At 8 a.m. the other 2 Sections which had returned to billets in the early dawn were fetched forward and set to work to construct 2 other strong Points, the ground having been cleared and mopped up by the Infantry as dawn broke. At 14.30 hours the ground being reconnoitred, and it being perfectly obvious that the enemy were retreating and no expectation of counter-attack the 2 Sections were ordered off the strong points they were constructing back to billets and stand by to move forward. On return to Advance Bde. H.Q. it was found that an order had been issued to move forward to MALINCOURT WOOD and prepare water supply in Malincourt. The Company moved forward and bivouaced in the quarry in T 4d. arriving at 23.00 hours. Casualties during the day - Lieut. Dickinson wounded.	Craxxxxfr
	9		Coy. at Malincourt occupied during day repairing crater at T 5a.2.4	
	10		Coy. completed repairs to above crater.	
	11		Coy. moved forward to ELINCOURT and undertook preparation of H.Q. for V Corps.	
	12		Coy. worked on Corps H.Q.	
	13		do.	
	14		do. Evening Coy. marched to BERTRY. No.4 Section marched via ELINCOURT, stayed one night there and repaired the shed for Divisional Surplus Kit store. They arrived on evening of 15th instant. In the evening a route was reconnoitred by the O.C. with Lieut.Griffiths for a cross country track and crossings across the river Selle to take Artillery and horsed transport.	
	15		No.4 Section arrived from ELINCOURT 13.00 hours. No.3 Section moved forward to TROISVILLES taking over maintenance of the crossings of the river Selle in the Divl. area from the 151st Field Co.R.E. No.1 Section, with No.4 Section when they arrived, worked on preparation of Divl.	

Army Form C. 2118.

WAR DIARY
or
INTELLIGENCE SUMMARY. 123rd FIELD COMPANY ROYAL ENGINEERS.
(Erase heading not required.)

Instructions regarding War Diaries and Intelligence Summaries are contained in F. S. Regs., Part II. and the Staff Manual respectively. Title pages will be prepared in manuscript.

Place	Date	Hour	Summary of Events and Information	Remarks and references to Appendices
IN THE FIELD	1918 Octr. 15		Theatre. On the evening of 15th No. 3 Section worked on the repair to damaged river bridges and tank crossing of the river Selle at K 16c.05.60 and approach thereto was reconnoitred by O.C. and Tank Officer. Lieutm Doyle with 9 men of No. 4 Section thereupon took an accurate section. The crossing and broken bridge in K 22a.70.05 was also reconnoitred and decided upon as a good alternative to the above route if necessary, with a little improving. Above Map Ref. Sh. 57b N.E (1/20,000)	C
	16		Lieut. Doyle with Nos. 1 and 4 Sections picked material, prepared and carried well on with the tank crossing of the river Selle; material being carried down in Pontoon wagons to the neighbourhood of S 21b.0.7 and thence by carrying party of 14th R.W.F. These 2 Sections worked 23 hours this day and night continuously, of which the last 8 hours the men were wading breast high in water. All Infantry posted on the river had been withdrawn to a distance of approximately 150 yards on our side in order to facilitate bombardment and discharge of gas. The enemy had approached very closely and work was carried out under persistent shelling M.G. fire and sniping. No. 3 Section with help of carrying party from 17th R.W.F. prepared damaged bridge and brought material for one cork float bridge across the Selle down to the neighbourhood of K 15b.3.6.	Sketch appendix A description appendix A
	17		No. 4 Section carried on with tank bridge. No. 1 Section under Lieut. Middleton with carrying party of 52 O.R. from 17th R.W.F. erected a cork float bridge across river Selle at S 16c.3.5. No 3 Section with carrying party of 18 men 17th R.W.F. erected one Float Bridge at K 15b.3.6 and repaired No. 11 Bridge which had been broken by shell fire. Through an error in the transport, only 2 bridges were erected this night in lieu of 5. During the evening of the 18th No. 4 Section completed tank bridge. On the morning of the 20th both tanks who attacked crossed this bridge without any difficulty also returned over it. No.4 Section also erected 4 foot bridges over river Selle in K 16c. No. 1 Section completed 3 foot bridges over the river in K 22a. No. 3 Section was employed on repair of existing bridges. Casualties - 1 O.R. wounded. Stores were taken down to K 21b. by transport. A carrying party of 108 men 17th R.W.F. was	C
	18			

Army Form C. 2118.

WAR DIARY
or
INTELLIGENCE SUMMARY.   123rd FIELD COMPANY
ROYAL ENGINEERS.

(Erase heading not required.)

Place	Date	Hour	Summary of Events and Information	Remarks and references to Appendices
IN THE FIELD	1918 Oct.			
	19		employed. The night was exceedingly light, the moon being full and no clouds: there was a slight mist. There were some casualties amongst the Infantry carrying party. On the whole the night was peaceful except for M.G. fire. Work was covered by covering party from 115th Inf. Brigade. During the evening tapes were laid out for all the bridges and number boards put out by Nos. 1 and 3 Sections to the road running through K 15a. c. and d. and K 21b. No. 3 Section did repairs to existing bridge where damaged. No. 4 Section and Section from 151st Co.R.E. prepared a girder bridge 28 ft. span to erect as a light Artillery Bridge over river Selle, and also prepared decking and timbers to convert existing tank crossing into a bridge to take Artillery. Late in the morning orders were received that the tank crossing was to be converted to take tanks as well as Artillery on the 20th inst. Lieut. G.S.Morgan returned from leave.	✓ ✓
	20		At 02.00 hours the Coy. assembled at the forward Bridging Dump J 30c.3.8 the following bridges being also prepared ready to put up across the Selle as opportunity permitted. 2 Pontoon Bridges, one superstructure for tank bridge, one 28 ft. span girder bridge. These were loaded on 4 Pontoon wagons, 1 G.S. wagon ready to move forward when required. Zero hour was 02.00. O.C.Coy. remained in K 25c. where were grouped H.Q. of both attacking Infantry Brigades, both Brigades R.F.A. and the Divl.M.G.Bn At 05.00 hours report being received the Infantry were well on way to final objective the route was reconnoitred forward and the valleys seeming clear of shelling except for harrassing fire, the pontoon bridge and the tank bridge were ordered forward with 1 and 4 Sections. The Sections moved forward to the river without incident. The heavy rain during the night had rendered the ground extremely soft and 10 horses had to be put into each wagon to move it forward and then with great difficulty. The enemy was using harrassing fire on the track in the neighbourhood of K 30 and 3 On arrival in the valley the enemy put down a barrage on the river. In spite of this the wagons went right up to the site, were unloaded and got clear away.	

A5834 Wt. W4973 M687 750,000 8/16 D.D. & L.Ltd. Forms/C.2118/13.

Army Form C. 2118.

WAR DIARY
or
INTELLIGENCE SUMMARY.

123rd FIELD COMPANY
ROYAL ENGINEERS.

(Erase heading not required.)

Place	Date	Hour	Summary of Events and Information	Remarks and references to Appendices
IN THE FIELD	1918 Oct. 20		The pontoon bridge and tank bridge were proceeded with in spite of heavy shell fire. The pontoon bridge was completed by 11.30 hours in spite of Lieut. Middleton and 8 men, out of a total of 21 for the two sections, having become casualties. The C.R.E. came on the site and it was decided that as the remaining men might become casualties any moment to move forward two sections of the 151st Co. R.E. and proceed with the erection of one more pontoon bridge as/at the tank bridge; also these sections were to reconnoitre and improve the track across the Railway into K 16b. Meanwhile the remains of Nos. 1 and 4 Sections carried on with the erection of the tank bridge under Lieut. Doyle. The 2 Sections of the 151st Coy. arrived and put under the orders of Lieut. Doyle. A second pontoon bridge with 2 pontoons also running the gauntlet of harrassing fire all along the track and heavy barrage in the valley. The pontoon bridge was completed by the 2 Sections of the 151st Coy., they also completed the track from the Bridge sites to K 16b.6.4, the route having been reconnoitred and chosen by Lieut. Doyle. The 2 Sections of the 123rd Coy. without assistance completed the tank crossing into a bridge capable of taking tanks and all traffic. It was doubtful at the time whether the crossing of this bridge by tanks would not destroy it for Artillery use, and it was so reported: but on the 21st inst. 4 tanks cross this bridge without damaging it. Meanwhile No. 3 Sect. had provided a maintenance party of 5 men under Sergt. Ferris to remain down in the river valley all night and keep open any essential bridges that might be damaged; the remainder of the section standing by to move & forward in the early morning and complete any more extensive repairs required. This maintenance party although gassed successfully carried out its task of repairing the bridges hit, (in one case a bridge being hit four times but kept open for traffic) with the exception of one bridge which was totally destroyed by shell fire. Casualties - Lieut. Middleton wounded 1 O.R. Killed, and 2 O.R. wounded. On the evening of the 20th Nos. 1 and 4 Sections returned to billets, No. 3 Section remaining there to carry on maintenance of the bridges.	
	21	14.00 hours	At 14.00 hours No. 3 Section, having incurred further casualties, was relieved by 151st Co. who undertook maintenance of bridges. Casualties	

Army Form C. 2118.

WAR DIARY
or
INTELLIGENCE SUMMARY.

123rd FIELD COMPANY
ROYAL ENGINEERS.

(Erase heading not required.)

Place	Date 1918	Hour	Summary of Events and Information	Remarks and references to Appendices
IN THE FIELD	Oct. 21		1 O.R. Killed 1 O.R. Wounded. Lieut. Morgan to Hospital.- Sick.	
	22		3 Sections employed on improving approaches to the 3 Artillery bridges.	
	23		Company rested. No. 1 Section moved to MONTAY and undertook maintenance of bridges	
	24		Nos. 3 and 4 Sections and 'B' Echelon moved to TROISVILLES, stopping the night in billets.	
	25		Company (less No. 2 Section and 'B' Echelon) moved to FOREST, No. 1 Sect joining the Coy. as it marched through MONTAY. 'B' Echelon moved to MONTAY.	
	26		Company (less No.2 Section) moved to POIX DU NORD, coming under orders of 115th Brigade. Horse Lines did not move. One Section of 124th Field Co.R.E. moved up to POIX DU NORD and came under orders of O.C. 123rd Field Co. for work. Orders received from 115th Brigade that 123rd Co. were to work in Left Battalion area with 17th R.W.F. in consolidating the main line of resistance, under orders of their C.O In the evening O.C. with officers reconnoitred the line the Infantry were holding. This consisted of a series of outposts on the eastern slope of a slight ridge running northwards from the eastern side of ENGLEFONTAINE. It was decided to run a belt of wire along the western slope of this ridge to form an obstacle in front of a position on the reverse slope of the ridge which should lend itself admirably to defence.	
	27		Three Sections of 123rd Co. with one Section 124th Co. wiring the line above reconnoitred. One single four-strand fence of wire was run out along the line reconnoitred, the wire being put as far as possible on existing hedges and fences, this being and extremely close country.	

Army Form C. 2118.

WAR DIARY
or
INTELLIGENCE SUMMARY.

128rd FIELD COMPANY
ROYAL ENGINEERS.

(Erase heading not required.)

Place	Date	Hour	Summary of Events and Information	Remarks and references to Appendices
IN THE FIELD	Oct. 28			
	29		Under orders of G.O.C. 115th Brigade four Sections wiring in the Infantry Outposts where necessary; about 600 yards of wire was put out in front of these.	
	30		115th Brigade were relieved by 114th Brigade. Sections went up to complete wiring of outpost line. On arrival forward it was found that the Infantry had already wired in their own outposts, so work was carried on with improvement of wire on the reverse slope position. There was much hostile shelling and Machine Gun fire. Work executed under great difficulties. The second belt of wire was carried on with, about 600 yards done across the Battalion front. Casualties - Lieut. C.W.Griffiths Wounded 1 O.R. of 124th Coy. Lieut. W.Dickinson rejoined Company.	
	30		Second wire fence on Battalion front completed.	
	31		Company moved to HARPTREE MILL and came under orders of C.R.E. section of 124th Cov. rejoined their Company.	

A.A. Pusey
Major RE.
O/C 128rd FIELD COMPANY
ROYAL ENGINEERS.

To accompany War Diary of 123. Field Co. R.E. - October 1918

Appendix "A"

REPORT ON CONSTRUCTION OF CRIB BRIDGE ERECTED OVER RIVER
SELLE AT K 16c.05.45 (Sheet 57b.) to CARRY LARGE TANKS
34 Tons.

A reconnaissance was carried out with a Tank Officer on the night of the 15th October, for deciding Tank route to the River and site of crossing.

An accurate section of the river bed was taken the same evening and it was decided that a crib would be the most suitable means of crossing.

It being most essential that the bridge should not be seen in daytime by the enemy, it was decided to construct it so that the top of the bridge should finish about 5" below the water level. After the tanks (which were to go over before zero) had crossed, it was built up to the bank levels and then used as an Artillery Bridge.

On the 16th plans were prepared and necessary material collected. Owing to the close proximity of the enemy (the river being in No. Man's land) it was necessary to do away with all hammering. Sleepers were drilled at each corner and those used for cross sleepers were prepared so as to take a 1½" dia. iron rod. Struts from either bank were also secured as per sketch, the sleepers in this case being bolted together

On the afternoon of the 16th the whole structure was fixed up on dry land, and marked with paint in order to see that all was in working order. On the evening of the 16th the material was taken forward in wagons to within 600 yards of the enemy over the forward slope where it was unloaded and carried to the site by a carrying party of 40 men.

The bolts were fixed into position and the first two layers of cribbing threaded on, on the bank of the river. Ropes were attached that this part was launched into the river, 1½" planking was fixed on the bottom crib so as to allow the sinking of metal which consisted of pieces of iron rails, to be retained in the crib. The top sleepers were threaded into position in the water and being sunk into position by rails.

Sheet 2.

On the first night the actual crib was completed so as to be 5" below water level. The work was delayed somewhat by hostile shelling, seveal shells falling within a radius of 30 yds. of the bridge. Machine Gun fire was also directed on to the bridge. Very lights falling within a few yards of the water.

The night of the 17th was occupied in fixing struts to E. and W. banks. On the night of the 18th the distance pieces were nailed in position and bridge completed.

The number of sappers employed were :-

    First night - 30 sappers
    Second " - 11 do.
    Third " - 5 do.

Bridge was completed in 30 hours before Zero.

The Bridge took the tanks quite successfully.

After Zero the crib was raised and bridge converted into a heavy traffic bridge which took over 4 34 tons Tanks on the following day.

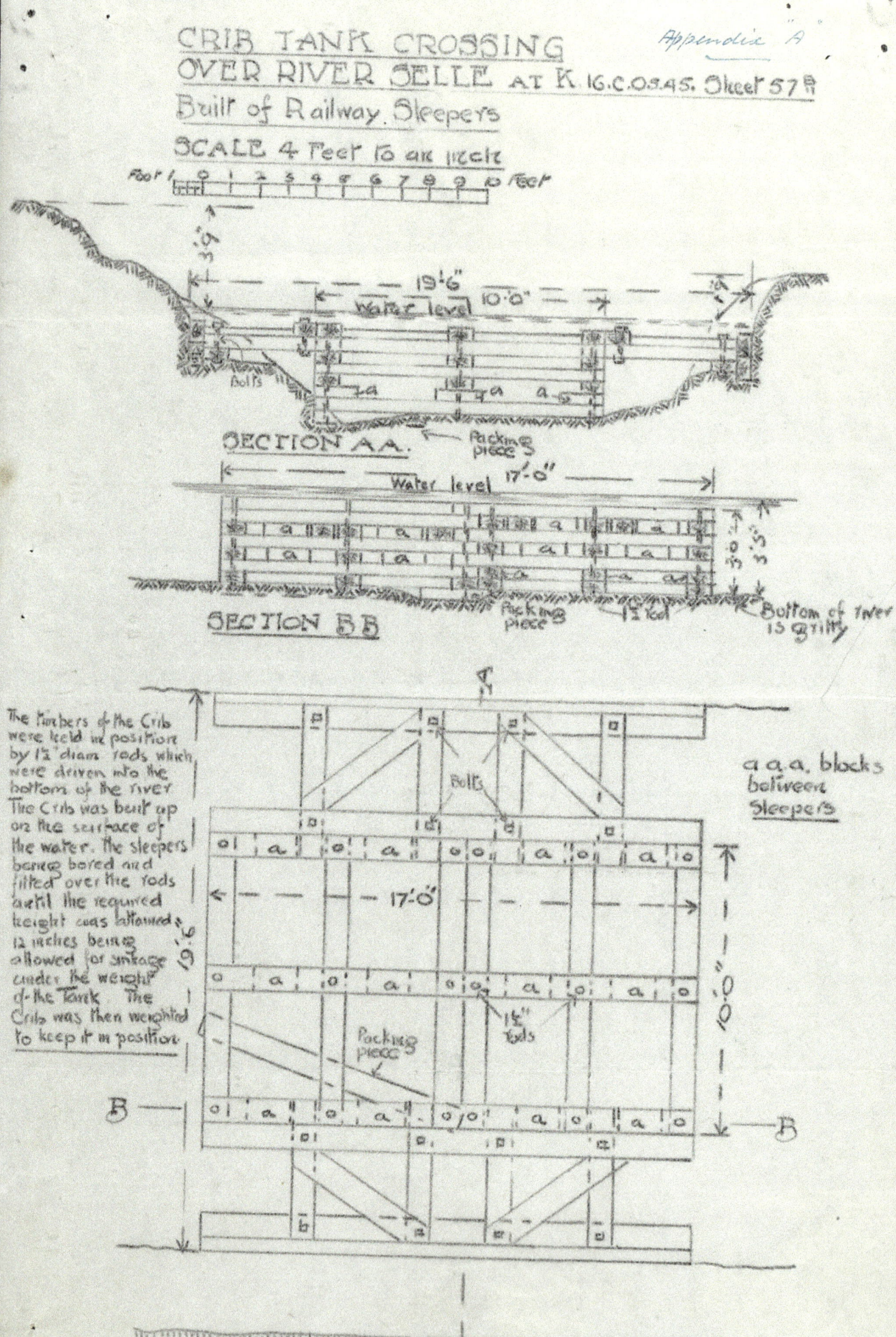

Secret.

Original War Diary

November 1st to November 30th
1918

_____

123 Field Company R.E.

Army Form C. 2118.

WAR DIARY
or
INTELLIGENCE SUMMARY.

123rd FIELD COMPANY
ROYAL ENGINEERS.

(Erase heading not required.)

Instructions regarding War Diaries and Intelligence Summaries are contained in F.S. Regs., Part II. and the Staff Manual respectively. Title pages will be prepared in manuscript.

Place	Date	Hour	Summary of Events and Information	Remarks and references to Appendices
Field	Nov 1		Sgt.J.Reid, Spr.W.J.Aitken, Drivers R.Westaway & T.W.Hopkins awarded M.M.	
	2		At Harples Mill E.21c.4.4. (Sheet 57b) Cleaning up.	
	3		do. Cleaning equipment and overhauling, Company Stores. Company inspection parade under O.C. 10 hours. O's.C.Conference at C.R.E.Office 14.15 hours.	
	4		do. Drawing R.E.Stores and materials for Coy. Dump. Loading Pontoon and Trestle Wagons at Horse Lines. Major Pressey M.C. reported to C.R.E's Office to act as Asst. C.R.E. 08.45 hours Coy. standing by for orders. 38 Div. attacked. Field Coys. under orders of C.R.E. Coy. move to ENGLEFONTAINE at 10.00 hrs. Orders received from C.R.E. at 12.45 hours that Coy. should billet at ENGLEFONTAINE. Lt. A.G.Doyle to Hospital - sick. Coy. employed on crater at A.10a.8.0. (Sheet 57b) A diversion for horse transport was first made around the crater and afterwards work proceeded on crater itself. Road to be made passable for single M.T. as soon as possible. Horse transport proceeded by diversion throughout the day.	
	5		04.45 hours Company paraded for work on crater at A.10a.8.0. (Sheet 57b) Work carried on throughout day. "B" Echelon moved from MONTAY to Harpies Mill.	
	6		Completed work on crater at A.10a.8.0, afterwards employed cleaning roads from A.3b.5.5. to Cross Rds at A.10a.8.3.	
	7		Coy. paraded 06.00 hours - moved to RIBAUMET C.2a.8.4. (Sheet 57a) arrivg 12.30 hours. Sections moved forward for work on crater in PETIT MAUBEUGE C"4d.75.75. (Sheet 57b) Road at first cleared around lip of crater and made passable for single transport. Coy. moved to billets at LEVAL for single transport. Coy. Moved to C.10c.70.75 - B Echelon arriving 22.30 hours.	
	8		Work on roads from Cross Rds at C.4d.75.75 to C.5c.5.0. cleaning rds and repairing Culvert at C.5c.25.40.	
	9		Work on culvert near DOULERS at D.11d.2.0. (Sheet 57b) A culvert of logs was made and excavation filled in and made passable for horse transpt.	
	10		Work continued on completion of road at D.11d.2.0. and made good for double "M"T. Company moved to E.1b.4.3. (Sheet 57b) Sgt.W.R.Ferris awarded bar at M.M.	
	11		Coy. standing by for orders. Message received from C.R.E. that hostilities cease 11.00 hours. Coy. employed on cleaning rds from E.7b.6.0. (Sht 57A) to W.19b.4.0. (Sht 51) 11 Lt. N.L.Hammond and 11 Lt. M.C.Ray Joined Unit.	
	12		07.30 hours Coy. moved to billets at AULNOYE U.29b.0.1. (Sht 51) and	

Army Form C. 2118.

WAR DIARY
or
INTELLIGENCE SUMMARY.

123rd FIELD COMPANY
ROYAL ENGINEERS.

(Erase heading not required.)

Place	Date Nov	Hour	Summary of Events and Information	Remarks and references to Appendices
Field	13		commenced work atonce at Divisional Theatre U.29b.2.3. Major H.A.S. Pressey rejoined unit.	
	14		AULNOYE. Work continued on Divisional Theatre.	
	15		do. do.	
	16		do. and renovating Coy. Transport.	
			do. 2 Sections collecting Bridging equipmt from Dumps near Canal de Sambre. 2 Sections cleaning up.	
	17		Aulnoye. Coy. attended Divisional Commanders Church Parade at 11.00 hrs. In afternoon football matches arranged but cancelled and work continued on Divisional Theatre. Major Pressey proceeded on leave. Capt. North assumed Command.	
	18		AULNOYE. 2 Sections working on Divisional Theatre, AULNOYE. 2 Sections employed on salving Gun limbers and G.S.wagon from Sanal de Sambre.	
	19		AULNOYE. 3 Sectns work on Coy. transport. 1 Sectn completed salvage of Gun Limbers and G.S. wagon and returned to D.A.D.O.S. 38 Div. Afternoon - Recreation.	
	20		AULNOYE. O's.C.Conference with C.R.E. at 124 Coy's Billet. 3 Sectns work on Div. Theatre. 1 Sectn repairing railway crossing at U.29a.9.2 (Sheet 51)	
	21		AULNOYE. 3 Sectns work on Div. Theatre at BERLAIMONT. 1 Sectn renovating Coy. transport. O's.C.Conference at C.R.E's	
	22		4 Sections work on Div. Theatre, BERLAIMONT until 11.30 hrs. Coy. marched to BERLAIMONT at 13.30 hrs arriving 14.30 hours and occupied Billets in U.31c. (Sheet 57b)	
	23		Sectns working on Div. Theatre, BERLAIMONT. O's.C.Conference at C.R.E's Office.	
	24		BERLAIMONT. Company employed cleaning and packing transport. Company training. Lieut. A.G.Doyle awarded M.C. No.428610 Sapper J.T.Cotton awarded D.C.M.	
	25		Inspection of Company and Transport by G.R.E. 38tn Divn.	
	26		Inspection of Company and transport by G.O.C. 38th Divn. and presentation of Honours and Awards - Three Field Coys. and Pioneer Bn.	
	27.		Company training.	

Army Form C. 2118.

WAR DIARY
or
INTELLIGENCE SUMMARY.

123rd FIELD COMPANY ROYAL ENGINEERS.

(Erase heading not required.)

Instructions regarding War Diaries and Intelligence Summaries are contained in F. S. Regs., Part II. and the Staff Manual respectively. Title pages will be prepared in manuscript.

Place	Date	Hour	Summary of Events and Information	Remarks and references to Appendices
In the Field	1918 Nov 28		Company Training. 14 animals drawn from Remount Depot to make up deficiencies.	
	29		Company training. Received orders to move to QUERRIEU area (HENENCOURT TRAINING AREA).	
	30		Company training. Packing wagons ready to move on 1st December.	

Smith
Captain R.E
O.C. 123rd Field Co. R.E

Secret.

Original War Diary -
December 1918.

123 Field Coy. Royal Engineers
38 (Welsh) Division.

31-12-1918

A.M.J. Pursey
Major R.E.
O.C. 123rd Co R.E.

WAR DIARY
or
INTELLIGENCE SUMMARY.

(Erase heading not required.)

Army Form C. 2118.

Instructions regarding War Diaries and Intelligence Summaries are contained in F.S. Regs., Part II. and the Staff Manual respectively. Title pages will be prepared in manuscript.

Place	Date 1918	Hour	Summary of Events and Information	Remarks and references to Appendices
BERLAIMONT	Dec 1	09.00 hours.	Horse Transport with Mounted personnel and 12 cyclists (1/Lt Hammond in command) left BERLAIMONT and proceeded to FRANVILLERS by march route via NEUVILLY etc. Lt. Dickinson attached to G.R.E. 38 Div for duty	
do	2	10.00 hours.	Coy. Hdqrs and dismtd personnel, with details of 115 Infy Bde att. (Capt Worth in command) left BERLAIMONT for FRANVILLERS proceeding to ENGLEFONTAINE by motor buses. Billeted night of 2nd at ENGLEFONTAINE.	
SALESCHES	3	08.00 hours.	Coy. Hdqrs, dismtd personnel etc. marched to SALESCHES and entrained for VILLERS BRETTONEUX; night 3/4th spent in train.	
VILLERS BRETTENEUX	4	15.15 hours.	Coy. Hdqrs dismtd personnel etc. detrained at VILLERS BRETTENEUX and marched to billets at FRANVILLERS. No casualties occurred during change of station BERLAIMONT - FRANVILLERS	
FRANVILLERS	5		Dismounted portionf Unit resting at FRANVILLERS. Mounted portion with Horses and Transport arrived FRANVILLERS 11.00 Hours. No casualties occurred with mounted men, horses and transport during march route BERLAIMONT - FRANVILLERS. O.C. Unit visited sites of work to be carried out by Unit at WARLOY and BAIZEAUX. Works at Nos. 1 and 2 Camps, WARLOY" taken over from Lieut Holman, 546 Field Coy. R.E.	
do	6		Nos. 2 & 3 Sectns, with transport, marched to Nos. 1 and 2 Camps, WARLOY" respectively and billeted in huts on Camp site. No. 4 Section with transport marched to BAIZEAUX and billeted in Prisoners of War Hutment Camp No. 1. No. 1 Section employed in preparing billets at FRANVILLERS. Drawing stores and materials from COLINCAMPS with Motor Transport. L/Cpl Wenham W.E. and Sapper Raymond W.H. awarded Military Medal 38 Div Order 4683 dated 3.12.18.	
do	7		Nos. 2,3 and 4 Sections employed on preparing Hutment Camps for 38 Div. at WARLOY. 200 German prisoners emplyd with Sectns.	

Army Form C. 2118.

WAR DIARY
or
INTELLIGENCE SUMMARY.
(Erase heading not required.)

Instructions regarding War Diaries and Intelligence Summaries are contained in F. S. Regs., Part II. and the Staff Manual respectively. Title pages will be prepared in manuscript.

Place	Date 1918	Hour	Summary of Events and Information	Remarks and references to Appendices
FRANVILLERS	Dec 8		Sunday. Check parade 9.30 hours. Major H.A.S. Pressey M.C. returned from leave and assumed Command of Coy.	C/
do	9		No. 2 Section. Work on No. 1 Camp. WARLOY.	C/
do	10		3 " " do. 2 " do.	C/
do	11		4 " " do. 1 " do.	C/
do	12		1 " " do. Coy billets and baths at FRANVILLERS.	C/
			do. do. do.	C/
			do. do. do.	C/
			Headquarters and No. 1 Section moved to WARLOY. No. 4 Section moved from BAIZIEUX to FRANVILLERS. Nos. 2 and 3 Sections. Work on Nos. 1 and 2 Camps respectively.	C/
WARLOY	13		No. 1 Section. Work on Horse standings for R.A.M.C. and patching up barns. Nos. 2 and 3 Sections. Work on Nos. 1 and 2 Camps respectively. No. 4 Section. Work on Battn. billets at FRANVILLERS.	C/
do	14		do.	C/
do	15	09.00 hrs.	Check parade. Company rested.	C/
do	16		Work as for 13th.	C/
do	17		do. Workshop started at WARLOY for making furniture.	C/
do	18 & 19		do.	C/
do	20		do. Lieut. Doyle returned from Hospital.	C/

Army Form C. 2118.

WAR DIARY
or
INTELLIGENCE SUMMARY.
(Erase heading not required.)

Place	Date	Hour	Summary of Events and Information	Remarks and references to Appendices
WARLOY	Dec. 21		Work as for 20th. Horse standing completed; No. 1 Section commenced work on 113 Brigade H.Q. VADENCOURT.	
do	22		do. Half days work.	
do	23		No. 1 Section. Work on 113 Bde H.Q. VADENCOURT. Nos. 2 & 3 Sections. Nos. 1 and 2 Camps, WARLOY. No. 4 Section. Bn Billets, FRANVILLERS. Capt. North proceeded on leave.	
do	24		Work as for 23rd.	
do	25	09:00 A.M. 13.30	Company Church Parade, WARLOY. Company Christmas dinner in WARLOY Schoolroom.	
do	26		Work as for 23rd.	
do	27		do.	
do	28		do. Nos. 2 and 3 Sections and Mounted Troops moved into fresh billets, WARLOY.	
do	29		do. 113 Infantry Bde marched into Billets.	
do	30		do.	
do	31		do.	

Secret.

Original
War Diary — Jan. 1919.

123 Field Coy. Royal Engineers
38 (Welsh) Division

Jan 1919

Army Form C. 2118.

WAR DIARY
or
INTELLIGENCE SUMMARY.
(Erase heading not required.)

Instructions regarding War Diaries and Intelligence Summaries are contained in F. S. Regs., Part II. and the Staff Manual respectively. Title pages will be prepared in manuscript.

Place	Date 1919	Hour	Summary of Events and Information	Remarks and references to Appendices
WARLOY	Jan. 1		No. 1 Section. Work 113 Bde H.Q. VADENCOURT; also making furniture in R.E. workshop, WARLOY.	
	2		do. Work on No. 1 Camp, WARLOY.	
	3		do. do. " do.	
	4		do. Work on Infantry Billets etc. FRANVILLERS.	
	5		do. do.	
	6		do. do.	
	7		do. do. (Half day)	
	8		No work.	
	9		Work as for 3rd inst. Lieut. Doyle A.G. on leave to U.K. for 14 days.	
	10		do. 2/Lieut. Hannom att. 124 Field Coy. R.E.	
	11		do. (½ day) Capt. North returned from leave.	
			do. Lieut. Dickinson W. awarded M.C. D.R.O. 4742.	
			do. (½ day) Following demobilized ; 98009 Spr Worthington J.	
				62405 Cpl Burge H.
				62645 Spr Adams I.W.
				564428. Spr Seudell A.V.
				212632. Dr Chapman J.
	12		do.	
	13		Work as for 10th.	52773. S.a C.S.Morgan F.
				20233 Spr Snell W.T.
	14		do.	
	15		No. 1 Section. Commenced Dismantling bridge at CERISIS.	
			do. Work on No. 1 Camp.	
			do. do. No. 2 Camp.	
			do. Work on billets etc. FRANVILLERS.	
			(half days work) Following man demobilized ; 457150 Sapper Watson J.	

Army Form C. 2118.

WAR DIARY
or
INTELLIGENCE SUMMARY.
(Erase heading not required.)

Instructions regarding War Diaries and Intelligence Summaries are contained in F.S. Regs., Part II. and the Staff Manual respectively. Title pages will be prepared in manuscript.

Place	Date	Hour	Summary of Events and Information	Remarks and references to Appendices
WARLOY	Jan. 17 18 19		Work as for 15th. do. (Half day) Coy. resting.	
	20		Work as before. 11 Lieut. Hammond N.L. Course of Instruction. Following demobilized ;	470707. Spr Robinson W. 140174. Spr Jones W. 448671. Dr Davies W.S. 20937. A/Sgt Brown G. 324861. L/Cpl Keir J. to Gosport, England for 145749. Spr Smith H. 564103. " Kelland S.W. 234289. " Campbell W.
	21		do.	402827. " Anderson A. 217523. " Shotton W.F. 145943. " Fell M.H. 212232. " Esler A.G.
	22		do. (½ day)	145711. " Banks R. 62515. " Wellington G. 100062. Dr Hoy A.D.
	23 24 25		No. 1 Section moving Hangar from SENLIS to QUERRIEU. Lt. Doyle RE. from leave. Nos. 2, 3 and 4 Sectns as before. do. (½ day) Following demobilized ; do. (½ day)	62574 Cpl Lewis T. 145508 Spr Lewis W. 91681 " Jenkins T. 551093 " Coles A.G. 67481 " Richards L.G. 428610 " Cottam J.T.

Army Form C. 2118.

WAR DIARY
or
INTELLIGENCE SUMMARY.
(Erase heading not required.)

Instructions regarding War Diaries and Intelligence Summaries are contained in F. S. Regs., Part II. and the Staff Manual respectively. Title page will be prepared in manuscript.

Place	Date	Hour	Summary of Events and Information	Remarks and references to Appendices
WARLOY	26		Work as for 25th. Company resting. Major Pressey and Capt. North visited site for new Reception Camp at Heilly. Capt. North took over command of Company on Major Pressey being attached G.R.E. 38th Div. Following demobilized ;- 164962. Spr Davey G.S.S. 95749 L/Cpl Wenham W.F. 224452. Spr Williamson F.	
	27.		No. 1 Section commenced re-erecting hangar at QUERRIEU. Nos. 2 and 3 Sections. Work as before. No. 4 Section moved to new billets at HEILLY. 11 animals (Category "Y") to Bourdon Horse Camp for demobilization. 1Lt. Richardson H.J. on leave. Following demobilized :- 443001. Sgt Young E. 62568. L/Cpl Jones H.R. 82452. Dr Rosser O.M. 83618. Spr Innes J.	
	28		Nos. 1,2 and 3 Sections. Work as before. No. 4 Section. Erecting Reception Camp at HEILLY. Army Act read to Company by Capt. S.North. Sections 42 - 44 Following demobilized ;- 108096. Dr Peever R. 62811. Spr Smith W.H. 309268. Dr Moore R. 542243. Dr Callaway G. 213022. Spr Windsor T. 155585. Spr Carey E.	
	29		Work as for 28th. (½ day) 82431. Sgt Price R.G. 446974. Cpl Newby W. 82589. Cpl Thomas A. 97378. Spr Hinson A.E.	
	30 31		First half of iron rations in possession consumed.	

Secret

Unit 123 Field Coy RE

War Diary for month
of February

28/2/19

Army Form C. 2118.

WAR DIARY
or
INTELLIGENCE SUMMARY.
(Erase heading not required.)

Place	Date	Hour	Summary of Events and Information	Remarks and references to Appendices
WARLOY	Feb 1		Work on Camps ; ½ day. Nos. 1 and 2 Camps, WARLOY. Reception Camp, HEILLY. Following demobilizations ; 63508. C.Q.M.S. Thomas J.W. 147464. Dr Foster L. 22046. Spr Callaway G. 263951. " King F.	
	2		Resting. do. 154100. L/Cpl Andrew A.J. 108013. " Evans G. 146629. A/Sgt Ordish R. 352598. Pnr McCool J. 163021. Dr Hopkins T.W.	
	3		Work as above.	
	4		do. (½ day)	
	5		do.	
	6		d o. do. Prince of Wales visited Unit. Following demobilizations ; 396638. Spr Williams O.E. 217412. " Crick P.J. 57238. " Gomm L.F. 164946. " Briggs A.G.	
	7		do. 474223. 2/Cpl Rowntree C.H. 163120. Dr Gibbins J.	
	8		do. 92513. Spr Reed W.	
	9		Resting. 89825. " Percival H.	
	10		Work as before. 207830. " Ticehurst J. 69507. L/Cpl Jones G.T. 82401. Dr Jones T.	
	11		do. 426950. Spr West A.	
	12		do. (½ day) 434616. " Parry O.W. 10771. L/Cpl Johnson E.H.	
	13		do. 167361. " Wise T.A.	

Army Form C. 2118.

WAR DIARY
or
INTELLIGENCE SUMMARY.
(Erase heading not required.)

Instructions regarding War Diaries and Intelligence Summaries are contained in F. S. Regs., Part II. and the Staff Manual respectively. Title pages will be prepared in manuscript.

Place	Date	Hour	Summary of Events and Information	Remarks and references to Appendices
WARLOY	Feb 14/15		Work as before. 2 Lt. Richardson returned from leave. Following demobilizations ; 63542. Spr Dearman A.J. No. 2 Section moved billets, joining 534502. " Hepton W.H. No. 1 Section in large hut. Thaw precautions from 01.00 hours. do. 62731. " Pritchard W.A. Work as before. 67547. Dr Charles B.T.	
	16		Resting.	
	17		Work as before.	
	18		Work; Camps as before. Erecting hangar at Frenchencourt. Preparing Dump for R.A.S.C. at CONTAY.	
	19		Work. ½ Day.	
	20		Work as before. Following demobilizations ; 20315. S. & C.S. Power M. 420567. Spr Sturrock J.W.	
	21		do.	
	22		do. (Half day) Resting. 92518. A/L/Cpl Clemoligue.	
	23 to		Work as before. Following Demobilizations 27th 67540. C.S.M. Rogers T.H. 63626. L/Cpl Hughes G. 91682. Spr Williams D. Work at Contay 305203. " Gowler W.G. R.A.S.C. dump complet 24th 402743. Sgt Reid J.	
	28			

Confidential

War Diary of 123 Field Coy RE
for month of March. 1919.

31-3-19.

Army Form C. 2118.

WAR DIARY
or
INTELLIGENCE SUMMARY.

(Erase heading not required.)

Instructions regarding War Diaries and Intelligence Summaries are contained in F. S. Regs., Part II. and the Staff Manual respectively. Title pages will be prepared in manuscript.

Place	Date	Hour	Summary of Events and Information	Remarks and references to Appendices
Daours France.	March 1919			
	1		Summer Time commenced. Work - Nos. 1 and 2 Camps, WARLOY. Hangar - FRECHENCOURT.	
	2		Work - do. 11 Lieut. Ray proceeded on leave.	
	3		Coy. moved to billets at R.E.Dump, DAOURS. Rear parties left at WARLOY and FRECHENCOURT to complete works in hand. 1 'D' for dispersal.	
	4		Work on billets.	
	5		do. Major Pressey rejoined Unit. Coy. transport moved to Cadre Park, GLISSY. Guard of 5 O.R. provided.	
	6		Work - Billets, checking stores and cleaning transport.	
	7		do. do. Cycles returned to D.A.D.O.S. 38th Div.	
	8		Work - Billets, checking stores and cleaning transport.	
	9		No work. Following demobilizations : 44564 Spr Barlow T. 63576 " Morris C. 62456 " James A.P. 82446 L/Cpl Yarwood J. 82424 Dr Norman T.J. 277463 Spr Sumner E.F. 458659 F.Sgt Wood R. 44816 Spr Murrel W. 26821 " Towlson H. (Watford detail)	

WAR DIARY
or
INTELLIGENCE SUMMARY.
(Erase heading not required.)

Army Form C. 2118.

Place	Date	Hour	Summary of Events and Information	Remarks and references to Appendices
Daours. France.	March 1919 10		Dismantling nissen hut at DAOURS and re-erecting same at GLISSY for accommodation of stores.	
	11		do. do.	
	12		Baths. Major Pressey as Conducting Officer for dispersal draft to England. Capt. S.North took over Command.	
	13		Erecting Nissen Hut at Glissy. Following demobilizations :- 83988. 2/Cpl Gale W. 82457 Dr Sevenoaks W.S 67404. Dr Stowe W.E. 108006 Spr Davies E.H. 513380 Cpl. Rowe F.J. 59304 Spr Evans W. 62451 Dr Hurdidge I.T. 62808 Spr Rose R. 108037 Spr Williams	
	14		Nissen Hut at Glissy completed. 16 'Z' animals for dispersal.	
	15		Capt. North S. left to join 219 Field Coy. R.E. Lieut. Doyle A.G. assumed command. Following demobilizations :- 97724. Spr Seal F. 104081 2/Cpl Briggs J. 533574. " Piper P. 470692. Spr Burns J.T. 62635. 2/Cpl Owen G. 108026 " Owen D.E. 61621. Spr Youde C.H. 108015 Dr Jones R.W. 93514. " Davies T. 434553 Spr Charnley G.E.	
	16		No work.	
	17		Work on billets.	
	18		Party dismantling baths at VADENCOURT.	

Army Form C. 2118.

WAR DIARY
or
INTELLIGENCE SUMMARY.
(Erase heading not required.)

Instructions regarding War Diaries and Intelligence Summaries are contained in F. S. Regs., Part II. and the Staff Manual respectively. Title pages will be prepared in manuscript.

Place	Date March 1919	Hour	Summary of Events and Information	Remarks and references to Appendices
France	19		Work at Vadencourt Baths. 1 'Z' animal for dispersal. 2/Lt Ray returned from leave.	
	20		Work at Vadencourt Baths. Lt Ray left to join 458 Field Coy. R.E. 1 'Z' animal for dispersal. Following demobilizations :- 536244. Spr Thorne H.S. 62496. Sgt Richards G.F. 212553. " Clapson T.J. 67311. Cpl Down W.T. 217577. " Handley J. 450066. Spr Thomas J. 134880. " Dulley F.C. 450106. " Marsden S. 311994. " Oxley H.P. 446702. " Jones C. 140368. " Short W.E. 446953. Dr Davey G. 82419. " Martin R. 108095. Dr Parry D.J. 91721. " Wright V.S. 412616. Dr Hynd H. 446922. Cpl Milburn J. 198519. Dr Sanderson L.	
	21		Work at Vadencourt Baths.	
	22		do. completed.	
	23		No work. 1 'X' animal for dispersal.	
	24		Laying out stores at GLISSY.	
	25		do. 199579. Dr Sanderson L. (Watford detail) for disposal.	
	31		do. and checking.	

Army Form C. 2118.

WAR DIARY
or
INTELLIGENCE SUMMARY.
(Erase heading not required.)

Instructions regarding War Diaries and Intelligence Summaries are contained in F. S. Regs., Part II. and the Staff Manual respectively. Title pages will be prepared in manuscript.

Place	Date	Hour	Summary of Events and Information	Remarks and references to Appendices
Daours France	April 1919			
	1		Cleaning and Packing Stores at Glisy.	
	2		Major Pressey.H.A.S. returned from Leave	
	3		Cleaning and Packing Stores at Glisy	
	4		do	
	5		do	
	6		Major Pressey.H.A.S. left Coy to report to War Office	
			Coy taken over by Lieut Doyle.A.G.	
			Sergt Turner Demobilized	
	15		Work commenced on repairing damaged Gate in Amiens	
	16		do	
	17		do	
	18		do	
	19		Work finished at Amiens	
	24		Work commenced erecting O.Mess & N.C.Os Mess for Chinese Labour Coy near Daours	
	25		do	
	26		do	
	27		do	
	28		do	
	29		do	
	30		do	

WAR DIARY
or
INTELLIGENCE SUMMARY.
(Erase heading not required.)

123rd Field Co. R.E. Army Form C. 2118.

From 1st May to 7th June 1919.

Instructions regarding War Diaries and Intelligence Summaries are contained in F. S. Regs., Part II. and the Staff Manual respectively. Title pages will be prepared in manuscript.

Place	Date	Hour	Summary of Events and Information	Remarks and references to Appendices
Daours	May 1919			
	1		Erecting O.Mess & N.C.Os.Mess for Chinise Labour Company near Daours.	
	2		do	
	3		do	
	4		Lieut Dickinson.W. transfered to C.R.E.38th Div.	
	5		Work at Chinise Labour Coy.	
	6		Work completed at Chinise Labour Coy.	
	18		Following Demobilizations 324490 Sapper Bond.F.	
	24		Following Demobilization 167898 L/Cpl Bolton.J.A.	
	31		Following Demobilization Lieut Doyle.A.G.	

Analysed net of file
O/C 123rd Fd Co RE

Army Form C. 2118.

WAR DIARY
or
INTELLIGENCE SUMMARY.

Unit **123** Field Coy R.E.

(Erase heading not required.)

Instructions regarding War Diaries and Intelligence Summaries are contained in F.S. Regs., Part II. and the Staff Manual respectively. Title pages will be prepared in manuscript.

Place	Date	Hour	Summary of Events and Information	Remarks and references to Appendices
Daours	June 1919			
	1		Work on Billets.	
	2		do do	
	3		do do	
	4		Handing in Unit Equipment to I.O.S. Pouldnville	
	5		Clearing Billets	
	6		All releasable Personnel to V Corps Concentration Camp Savause for Demobilisation	
	7		All Retainable Personnel to C.R.E. 6th (Midland) Division (Army of the Rhine) Unit disbanded	

www.ingramcontent.com/pod-product-compliance
Lightning Source LLC
Chambersburg PA
CBHW080924230426
43668CB00014B/2190